becker&mayer! books

Woodstock

The 1969 Rock & Roll Revolution

ERNESTO ASSANTE

becker&mayer! books

TABLE OF CONTENTS

Opposite: The famous poster from the Woodstock festival, from August 15-17, 1969. The guitar and dove were an idea from the artist, Arnold Skolnick, who delivered the job in only five days.

Above: (Top) The first page of the *Daily News* from August 16, 1969, highlights the incredible chaos created by traffic generated by young people arriving in Bethel for the festival. (Bottom) The cover of the *Sunday News* from August 17, 1969, describes the "Hippies stuck in the mud."

Introduction

A dream, a myth, an exaggeration, a reality, a legend. Woodstock was this and much more. Not only a festival but "THE" festival. Not only a counterculture gathering in the sixties, but the highest point of a plan not written yet, to demonstrate that society and its rules could be changed. And especially the main gathering of the history of rock, the beginning of a new era for music.

No, it wasn't a dream; it really happened. Some might say it was all a myth, exaggerated by recollections and made colossal by the movies. In reality, you could say that it was a festival like all the others—actually worse than the others. There was a lot of mud, nothing worked, and thanks to the rain, the sound system was often more toward the lightning than the amplifier. Also, people did not have anything to eat or drink. Truly, everything was out of control.

However, it's exactly these elements that made Woodstock unique in history. Half a million young people accepted all of this and participated—not for an unmotivated spirit of support, but because they were in ecstasy. In other words, a spiritual, physical, and mental state that pushed everyone toward good, around the sharing, illumination, and the possibility that everything in some way finds a balance. And this ecstasy was created so that a balance could truly be found. It was the "Woodstock Nation," like activist and author Abbie Hoffman called it. It was lived by a population that wanted a different life, a different society, a different world. A nation without a flag or national anthem, a population without roots if not for those planted in the earth by freedom. A population with ideas, emotions, and passion—a population able to live for three days in impossible conditions, listening to fantastic music, without rules, without police, without money.

This event that we are recounting is, in other words, a fairy tale—with a happy ending. A fairy tale that could be told millions of times because as absurd as it sounds in today's world, for three days, it was reality. For three days, everything that you will read really happened.

Above: A group of artists from the Beat Generation sitting at a restaurant table. From left to right: poet Gregory Corso, with hat (1930–2001), painter and musician Larry Rivers (1923–2002), writer Jack Kerouac (1922–67), musician David Amram (1930), and poet Allen Ginsberg (1926–97).

BEAT, HIPPIE, YIPPIE, AND FREAK

Birth of a Counterculture

The long road to Woodstock began in 1958, when Jack Kerouac published *On the Road*, his most famous novel, and when a journalist from the *San Fransisco Chronicle*, Herb Cohen, coined the term "Beatnik." This last was used not only to define the poets from the Beat Generation but also the young who were tired of the rules and restrictions of American society from the 1950s, and for this reason, in a personal and nonpolitical way, they rebelled. Kerouac was one of the representatives of the Beat Generation, made up of a group of writers and poets that transformed rebellion into poetry and literature and, at the same time, tried to transform poetry and literature into life. These poets, scholars, and dreamers wanted to escape from conformity and routines to the commune, glorifying liberty and pleasure. Besides Kerouac there were Allen Ginsberg, William Burroughs, Lucien Carr, Gregory Corso, Gary Snyder, editor and poet Lawrence Ferlinghetti, Neal Cassady, and many others; conformists thought they were a group of stragglers, society's trash, and scoundrels who tried by any means to survive without too many rules. But it was truly the opposite. Author Federico Ballanti wrote, "Overstepping the rules causes fatigue and insecurity and is bad for your health. And it requires a lot of courage and persistence."

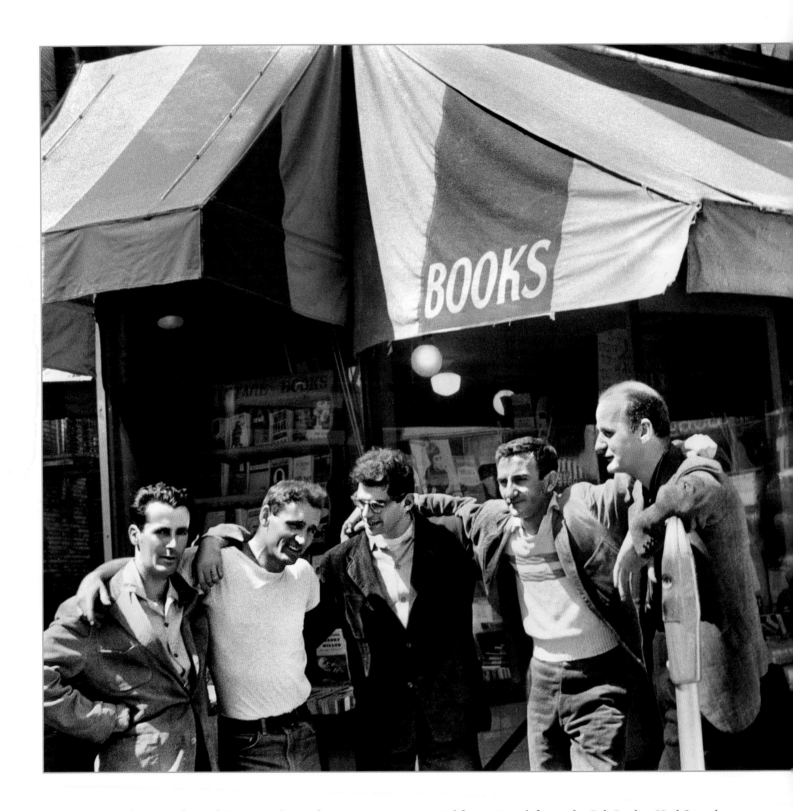

Above: A group of Beats in front of the City Lights Bookstore in San Francisco, California. From left to right: Bob Donlon, Neal Cassady, Allen Ginsberg, Robert LaVigne, and writer and editor Lawrence Ferlinghetti, bookstore owner. The picture is from 1956 and was shot by another Beat poet, Peter Orlowski.

The Beats tried everything for themselves: overindulgences and romances, madness and perditions, passion and sex, alcohol and desires. They were part of the first American generation that refused the American "dream" and they did not want to burn any of their individuality or their passion on the altar of a quiet life.

Allen Ginsberg, Jack Kerouac, and Lucien Carr were well known at Columbia University in New York. Little by little, Gregory Corso, William Burroughs, Neal Cassady, and Gary Snyder joined them, giving life to an "open" group that did not follow established rules. The Beats applied the rhythm, the beat and the length of the bebop phrasing to their style of writing. Kerouac with his "bop prosody" tried to assimilate his writing style to Charlie Parker's musical style; Ginsberg acted out his poems, adapting the sentences to his breath, applying the syncopation to the accentuation of the words. They are the fathers of the counterculture, even if they claimed what they were doing was not directly political; their rebellion was not aimed at changing the collective status quo, but only the one inside of each person. It was personal and individual. Their poems and wish for freedom were the fuse for the explosion of a new young culture at the dawn of the sixties.

There are two links between the Beat Generation and the one that followed: San Francisco inspired change with its pulsating heart, and Neal Cassady served as the inspiration for Kerouac's central character, Dean Moriarty, in *On the Road*.

San Francisco—the city in which Lawrence Ferlinghetti's bookstore, City Lights, around which a large part of the Beat adventure was developed—put in motion the young "revolution" that would directly bring on the three days of Woodstock. How did that happen? If we want to find musical roots, we could look to the Beach Boys and the magical vocals combined with pure fun that Brian Wilson and his brothers introduced at the dawn of the sixties. They brought together rock and roll, doo-wop, and more in an electrifying and adolescent form called "surf."

"On the Road"

Above: Writer Ken Kesey and the legendary Neal Cassady, who was immortalized in Kerouac's *On the Road*. They are talking aboard "Further," the bus belonging to the Merry Pranksters, during their arrival to New York on "the trip" of 1964.

In fairness, however, if we look closer, the scenario becomes more complex when Ken Kesey enters the scene. He was a writer and cultural provoker, the perfect son of the half-generation, "too young to be a Beatnik, and too old to be a hippie," as he loved saying about himself. Kesey had experimented with a very potent drug, LSD, when it was legal in the laboratories

of Sandoz and under the official supervision of the CIA for the program called MKUltra. The experience brought him to write a successful book, *One Flew Over the Cuckoo's Nest*, and it pushed him to change his life, moving from the suburbs of San Francisco to La Honda, where he began a sort of proto-hippie community during the first years of the sixties—the

Above: Chet Helms (with the beard), coordinator of the evening events at Avalon Ballroom in San Francisco, talks with some Merry Pranksters and with Ken Kesey about the organization of the Halloween party on October 31, 1966, themed as "Acid Graduation Ball."

Merry Pranksters. Kesey theorized that the free use of LSD would bring about an expansion in the collective conscience, pushing the world toward change. In 1964 he organized a trip from one coast to the other with the Merry Pranksters. "The trip" was with an old school bus, readjusted and decorated by the community, and renamed "Further." Neil Cassady drove the bus. It is here that the connection between past and future became evident. Kesey and his group were the organizers of the Acid Test in which LSD was distributed and live music was played inside theaters with light shows. They were "experiences" that Kesey thought were important to expand the field of consciousness and push the participants toward a different perception of reality.

In the following years, the youth culture changed in a radical way. The arrival of the Beatles caused a cultural explosion and the arrival of Bob Dylan demonstrated that songs were no longer just entertainment; they could have important content and social impact, with lyrics about peace and violence instead of only love and broken hearts. The youth of the nation were starting a movement, beginning with those at Berkeley University in California, led by Mario Savio. They were open to "blocking mechanisms" of power intended to stop the escalation of the Vietnam War, and putting everything up for discussion—institutions, including family, education, money, society, and each of its expressions—following the dream of a better and more just life. Some dreamed of changing the world. Others instead practiced change in a direct way. They were the hippies.

Above: Ken Kesey, with the microphone in hand, talks to Merry Pranksters about how to go "beyond acid" in one of the Californian Acid Tests.

Opposite: Youngsters dance during an Acid Test—parties where they consumed LSD—and helped with projection, live music, and theatrical performances.

They were the new generation of libertarians not willing to follow in the footsteps of their parents. These hippies considered Western culture to be corrupt, and in some way lost. They believed that human and social relationships should be discussed. They preached universal love and peace, they loved music, and they lived following a variety of shared rules. The first communities began to organize themselves in the middle of the sixties, while the Haight-Ashbury neighborhood in San Francisco became the place where a large number of the first hippies went to live. It was at that time that Chet Helms's Family Dog, the San Francisco Mime Troupe managed by Bill Graham, and the Diggers were born. They opened up the first "head shop."

Above: A theater built on the street in 1967 by the San Francisco Mime Troupe, a hippie theater group, managed by Bill Graham.

Opposite: The San Francisco Mime Troupe on the street during a rally at People's Park in Berkeley, California, 1969.

The first big gathering of this new generation was held in 1966 in San Francisco with the Trips Festival. This brought together rock musicians, poets, cultural agitators, activists, artists, and many ordinary youngsters who for the first time would all gather together. Some Merry Pranksters came alongside Stewart Brand. "I was the organizer for the Trips Festival in 1966. I was not born to be a coordinator. I was with the Merry Pranksters of Ken Kesey and I realized that they would have never had the ability to organize something like that. But it was the right moment to do it, to bring together everyone that was trying to do something, a big gathering of the whole group spread around the Bay Area. Kesey really liked the idea of the festival; it was the natural evolution of his Acid Test. But the Pranksters would have not been able to do something of the sort, so I got on the phone and started making phone calls to make it happen. It worked without a lot of problems, and to tell you the truth, without costing a lot either. We showed that it was

possible to act on and make a difference. No one could imagine that there were so many of us and all in the Bay Area. It was surprising for us and for everyone, and we understood that the movement was big, powerful, and fun. And it could show people things in a different way."

So from January 21–23, with the help of Bill Graham at Longshoreman's Hall in San Francisco, the Trips Festival was born, with bands of a caliber such as Grateful Dead, and Big Brother and the Holding Company. It was the visible beginning of the hippie counterculture; the moment in which all that had been buried for two or three years shockingly came to the light of day. Six million people danced and tried LSD. Like in the Acid Test, they lived an experience that brought together music, theater, and light shows.

Lysergic acid became illegal the following October, but instead of consumption going down, it went up exponentially throughout the United States and Europe. The "psychedelic" season opened, in which

Left: Timothy Leary and Neal Cassady, during their first meeting, in 1964, in Millbrook, New York, during the "magic trip" of Cassady and his Merry Pranksters.

Opposite: Timothy Leary on the stage, together with Allen Ginsberg, on December 6, 1966. They were on the Village Gate stage in New York during the last of three evenings titled, "Illumination of the Buddah," a "psychedelic multimedia celebration," put together along with Dick Alpert.

the main prophets were Timothy Leary and Richard Alpert. Both professors at Harvard, they started to experiment using lysergic acid with their students some years before. Because of this, in 1963, they were expelled from the university. During the same year, Leary, along with Ralph Metzner, wrote a book titled, *The Psychedelic Experience* in which he explained that "a psychedelic experience is a trip around new realms of consciousness. The dimension and the content of the experience does not have limits and its

characteristic connotations are the transcendence of verbal concepts, of temporary-space dimensions and of ego or identity." The new reality, the new music, and the circulation of LSD (attributed to Owsley Stanley, accomplice to the "chemical" and soundmaster of the Grateful Dead)—the drug synthesized by Albert Hoffman many years earlier—together with the refusal to conform to society and its rules, would bring on a new gathering: the Love Pageant Rally.

Human Be-in – Golden Gate Park

Left: Allen Ginsberg chants "Om" among the crowd of "Human Be-In" at Golden Gate Park in San Francisco, on January 14, 1967.

Above: Janis Joplin with her band, Big Brother and the Holding Company, on the New Year's Wail stage, January 1, 1967,

The rally took place October 6, 1966 (the same day that LSD was criminalized) at the Golden Gate Park in San Francisco, in the Panhandle—the part of the park that extends to the Haight-Ashbury zone. It became the hippies' neighborhood with stores, newspapers, and alternative structures. Allen Cohen and Michael Bowen organized the gathering. They were responsible for the *San Francisco Oracle*, the

"bible" of counterculture, born only one month before and the forefather of alternative newspapers, the "free press" that would construct the important fabric of disinformation all over the United States.

"We wanted to create a celebration of innocence," said Cohen, and the poster that announced the event asked people to bring flowers, incense, instruments, feathers, bells, drums, and costumes. The Grateful

Above: The stage of "Human Be-In" at Golden Gate Park in San Francisco is ready to host the Grateful Dead, on January 14, 1967.

Dead and Janis Joplin played, and Ken Kesey and the Merry Pranksters arrived on their bus. It was the precursor to the the first big, universal hippie gathering, the Human Be-In of January 1967, that introduced the long "Summer of Love" in San Francisco. Some tens of thousands of young people gathered on January 14, 1967, at the Golden Gate Park for a "gathering of the tribes," called by Leary, Alpert, Dick Gregory (comic actor and activist of the movement for civil rights), Allen Ginsberg, Lawrence Ferlinghetti, and Jerry Rubin. There were the dreamers and the hippies, activists and poets, and the rock era was ripe in San Francisco, with performances by Carlos Santana, Steve Miller, Jefferson Airplane, Big Brother and the Holding Company, Blue Cheer, the Grateful Dead, and Quicksilver Messenger Service.

Right: The Grateful Dead in concert at Human Be-In on January 14, 1967. American media emphasizes the big turnout of young people for the event that brought together a crowd between 20,000 and 30,000 altogether.

Above: A photo from a hippie gathering in 1967. The "blaze" is a liberating act to declare the "death of the hippies," emphasizing the end of the "Summer of Love" in San Francisco.

It was the beginning of an extraordinary year with the release of the Beatles' *Sgt. Pepper's Lonely Heart Club Band*, and of the debut recordings of the Doors and Jimi Hendrix. It was the year in which the world dressed in flower-power colors, the year in which the hippies (who had already staged a "funeral" in Haight-Ashbury some time before, just in case) became a topic of discussion in American households, especially ones in which children had decided to follow the "rules" that Timothy Leary had established at the Human Be-In: "Turn on, tune in, drop out." The hippies were spread out all over, not only in California or San Francisco (that represented the nondeclared hippie capital), and they discussed the entire system of American society, including money, family, education, the political system, and justice. They wanted to change the rules of civil coexistence, they preached free love and peace, they were environmentalists and hugely libertarians, and they were leaders of love, joy, creativity, and equality.

They didn't count on a complete revolution of the status quo, rather they practiced the revolution in their small communities created after having "given up everything." The communes were where they could live far from consumerism and rules. No money circulated among them; they opened free stores where trades were open, and they opened free clinics where you could be cared for at no cost. Meanwhile the lawyers of the new generation offered assistance to whomever needed it. Known as the Diggers, they prepared free lunches, the bands played for little or nothing, and above all, there were no leaders and no bosses; all that existed was the direct democracy, and the decisions were collective. The music became the universal medium for all of the dreams and desires. The music went above the confines of the genre, which was no longer pop, and its objective was not to conquer the charts, but to unite. Psychedelic art was the main goal.

"Turn on, Tune in, Drop out"

Left: Allen Ginsberg and Gregory Corso among youngsters gathered in Central Park in New York to celebrate the Easter Be-In, on May 26, 1967. Less structured compared to San Francisco, the event brought out 10,000 young people.

Above: A band plays during the "Summer Solstice Festival" at Golden Gate Park in San Francisco, in 1967. It is the official beginning of the Summer of Love, the summer that marks the hopes and dreams of an entire generation.

In the meantime, everything was in motion, even in London: Pink Floyd animated evenings at the UFO Club and held countercultural rallies like the "14 Hour Technicolor Dream." Carnaby Street had imposed its look everywhere, while rock dominated the scene. Anything seemed possible—even changing the world. The album that represented the moment more than any other was Sgt. *Pepper's Lonely Hearts Club Band,* with its visionary cover and its music that mixed East and West, avant-garde, and pop. This was the moment in time when the fuse was lit. It was the year in which Cassius Clay refused to go to Vietnam, and when Che Guevara was killed in October. That year, 1967, rock music became the official auditory pillar for the young culture and the entryway to the new world. Rock transformed itself into a tool so that even those who didn't live in San Francisco, or who did not grow out their hair, or who didn't think to practice the hippie life, felt like they were a part of the community and part of the movement.

Still, in 1967, a few weeks after the release of *Sgt. Pepper,* the first big rock festival in history happened at Monterey. The Monterey International Pop Music Festival lasted three days, from June 16 to 18, and hosted tens of thousands of people who came to listen to the Association, the Paupers, Lou Rawls, Beverly, Johnny Rivers, the Animals, Simon & Garfunkel, Canned Heat, Janis Joplin with Big Brother and the Holding Company, Country Joe and the Fish, Al Kooper, the Butterfield Blues Band, Quicksilver Messenger Service, Steve Miller Band, Electric Flag, Moby Grape, Hugh Masekela from South Africa, the Byrds, Laura Nyro, Jefferson Airplane, Booker T. & the M.G.'s, the legendary Otis Redding, Ravi Shankar, the Blues Project, Grateful Dead, Buffalo Springfield, the Who, Jimi Hendrix Experience and, to conclude, the Mamas & the Papas with frontman and festival organizer, John Phillips. Phillips—along with Lou Adler, Alan Pariser, and Derek Taylor—coordinated the music festival, together with main sponsors, including Paul Simon, and an honor committee made up of Brian Wilson, Donovan, Paul McCartney, Roger McGuinn, Smokey Robinson, Mick Jagger, Andrew Loog Holdam, and Chip Monck as stage manager and lights supervisor.

Also, in the audience there were many other musicians from that time period, such as Brian Jones.

Monterey Pop Festival

Above: The Who destroy their instruments that they used to perform with at the end of their set on the stage of the festival in Monterey, California, on June 18, 1967.

Above: Brian Jones from the Rolling Stones next to Nico from the Velvet Underground among the Monterey Festival Crowd, on June 18, 1967.

Opposite: Jimi Hendrix shows off during the Monterey Pop festival, June 18, 1967. At the end of his performance, he sets his Fender Stratocaster guitar on fire, a symbolic gesture in the history of rock.

"Be sure to wear some flowers in your hair"

It was the first time that the world of rock agreed with everyone, the first time the American bands and those of "swinging London" were together, and were all ready to perform without payment because the proceeds were donated to charity. Philips was also the author of "San Francisco," the song that served as the promotional "flier" for the festival. The song, sung by Scott McKenzie, childhood friend of Philips and his partner-in-adventure in Journeyman (with whom he made three albums and different singles), immediately became a worldwide success, selling more than seven million copies. The first verse of the song said, "If you go to San Francisco, be sure to wear some flowers in your hair," which then painted the revolution underway in delicate terms. "All over the country there is a strange vibration, people in movement, there is an entire generation with new explanations, people in movement." It was with this song that McKenzie went on stage at Monterey to accept his well-earned success. In the meantime, the song had become a huge international hit, reaching a wider and diverse audience. It became the popular theme of the hippie culture. Other history-making performances happened: the debut of Janis Joplin and Big Brother; the performances of Otis Redding and David Crosby, who would go on stage with Buffalo Springfield; the stage destruction by the Who; and the pagan ritual celebrated by Jimi Hendrix (that returned for the first time in America), setting fire to his guitar. Monterey showed to the world that rock was an extraordinary reality and the young movement was much bigger, more creative, and much more important than was thought to be at that time. The festival explained to the world that "the times were changing," as Dylan sang. A new complete culture was here, with its newspapers, fashion, books, music, macrobiotic food, Eastern religion, peace, and mind-expanding drugs. Monterey introduced the Summer of Love and millions of people from every part of the world wanted to be a part of it. The people were truly in movement everywhere, just like McKenzie sang.

"Two groups truly created the counterculture of the sixties," Stewart Brand, promotor of the Trips Festival of 1966, said. "The 'New Left' and all those that revolved around psychedelics, the hippies, and both would reach a very wide audience. The two groups did not communicate much. Kesey, for example, wanted nothing to do with those of the New Left. Essentially, they had legitimate reasons but they said things that could not be defended, such as, 'Mao is a great leader.' The distinction between the hippies and the New Left was rather clear-cut. There were also many points of contact over the years because reality was different for many young people: they would leave home, create communes for awhile, then they would get really bored because they felt that nothing around them was changing, so they returned back to the city and committed themselves to politics." The year 1968 arrived and, to the hippie logic, their "dropout." The activists responded with increasing aggression: if the world did not change and put "the flowers in the

cannons," another way needed to be attempted with politics, with a revolution. Politics captured the souls of youngsters in the United States and in the rest of the world with the battle for civil rights, the protest against the Vietnam War, the growth of "revolutionary" formations such as the Black Panther Party, the radicalization of SDS (Students for a Democratic Society), the French May, the political formations of the young from the extreme left in Italy, the search for freedom in Poland, and the student protests in Mexico, just to name a few examples. It was a radicalization that happened in the United States, also in response to the violence brought on by the killing of Martin Luther King Jr. in April, and the assassination of Robert Kennedy in June.

To bridge the hippies and the activists, the yippies came—the components of the Youth International Party founded by Abbie Hoffman and Jerry Rubin. The yippies were revolutionary and creative, psychedelic, and activists at the same time, capable of creating a big impact on the media with spectacular, peaceful, and surprising gestures, such as when they threw money at the traders of Wall Street or when they organized the "levitation of the Pentagon" to protest against the Vietnam War. The yippies—together with the National Mobilization Committee to End the War in Vietnam, the "MOBE"—decided to organize a huge rally, a Free Festival, in Chicago, during the Democratic Party Convention to nominate a pig named Pigasus the Immortal Pig, to be president of the United States.

However, the festival did not last. The police violently attacked the rallies, and several days of arguments and incidents were recorded. At the end, Jerry Rubin, Abbie Hoffman, Dave Dellinger, Tom Hayden, Ronnie Davis, John Froines, Lee Wiener, and Bobby Seale were arrested and accused of conspiracy and enticement for the revolt. The rally and the process became the subject of one of the most beautiful and famous songs by Graham Nash, called "Chicago," which became a classic by Crosby, Stills, & Nash. In the meantime, the rock festival began to evolve a little bit all over. Between 1968 and 1969, there were dozens like Wight in England; more in San Francisco, Los Angeles, Denver, and Atlanta; and in Bath and Hyde Park in London (with the Rolling Stones crying over the disappearance of Brian Jones). There were others in Seattle and Miami, the latter organized by Michael Lang, a producer who would shortly be headed toward Woodstock.

Left: Founded in 1966 in Oakland, California, the revolutionary organization of socialist inspiration, the Black Panthers, had the goal to free the African-American community from racial discrimination. Contrary to the nonviolent method, they preferred self-defense.

Above: Abbie Hoffman, one of the prominent personalities in American counterculture and leader of the Yippies, talks to the students at Columbia University, in New York, on March 13, 1968.

Left: Allen Ginsberg at Lincoln Park in Chicago, on August 25, 1968, during the rallies of protests held in concurrence with the democratic convention of that same year.

Above: Abbie Hoffman parades together with other demonstrators on August 30th, 1968, during one of the rallies organized to protest against the Vietnam War while the Democratic Party Convention was going on.

MICHAEL LANG

How to Organize the Most Famous Festival in the World

Michael Lang could write a manual for being a festival organizer, and encountering all of the negative conditions yet having wild success in spite of it. "Yes, nothing in the cards was in our favor but . . ." A month prior to the beginning of the festival, nothing positive was foreseen. Partly because twenty-five-year-old Lang had no experience, history, fame, or contacts—everything that, in theory, would have been necessary to organize the most important gathering in the history of music, one of the main cultural progressions in the last century, and one of the most fundamental culmination of events that would be necessary to define the world in the middle of the 1900s.

"I lived in Miami and organized several concerts, especially the Miami Pop Festival in which Jimi Hendrix was the headliner. That experience was enlightening; it was clear that the relationship that my generation had with music was different from the previous ones. So, it was decided to do something bigger. At the time, events called Sounds-Out were organized. They were peaceful, in the country, very calm. The people came and camped out if they wanted to stay the weekend. It seemed like the right time to listen to music, without police, supervision, tension. So the idea of a big event called Sounds-Out was put together."

The first "brick" added to Michael Lang's "construction" of Woodstock was from Artie Kornfield: "He was a music industry genius, but the albums were not like those of today, in a jacket and tie. I called him in the office to introduce a band that I was looking after at that time. I didn't have an appointment. I said that I was from his same neighborhood and he let me in. He was successful. He was in the business since the middle of the fifties, also as a musician. We became friends; he helped me when I didn't have any money for about a year and a half."

The next two bricks would arrive soon. Joel Rosenman and John Roberts were two guys from good families, with money to spend and the desire to do something different. They met on a golf course. One was a lawyer and the other began working in the financial market but neither of them liked that life, so much that they even tried to start a sitcom.

Right: Michael Lang, one of the four coordinators of the Woodstock festival, on the phone in one of the motel rooms that became the operative center of the Bethel organization.

In order to have an idea of what to invest in, in March of 1967, they decided to put an ad in the *Wall Street Journal*, that read, "Young men with unlimited capital looking for interesting and legitimate opportunities and business propositions." Seven thousand responded, most of them wrongdoers, but the announcement grabbed the attention of Lang and Kornfield. "Joel Rosenman and John Roberts were not part of the counterculture or of the music world; they were two rich guys in search of a business to invest in. We were all young and very different; John and Joel were regular guys. The relationship was not easy, especially at the beginning. Without their determination and their ability to manage business though, it would have been impossible to succeed. Artie and I were in contact with Joel and John because we wanted to make an offer to invest in the opening of a recording studio outside of New York, at Woodstock. They were not exactly convinced, but when I suggested that they have a launch party and that they invite Bob Dylan, they offered to do something bigger, thinking that it was better to invest in a festival rather than in a recording studio. They convinced themselves and we quickly got to work."

The idea to keep the concert at Woodstock was pleasing to everyone. It was a perfect location that was not far from New York City, "and thinking about Sounds-Out, it seemed to be the right place, also because there was a musician and artist community that lived in the area."

In reality, the festival would never get to Woodstock. The first location that the four of the "Woodstock Ventures" would find was more than forty miles from Woodstock. "We had pinpointed the place in the Howard Mills industrial park at Wallkill and we agreed on about $10,000.00. For us, it was done; we printed the poster, announcing the festival, and started working. But the citizenry understood that it was a big event. They were scared, and the permit that we received was revoked. We were truly in trouble because it was the beginning of June and we had signed contracts with artists. Now we did not have a place to hold the festival. Around the area there was Bethel and there was a motel called El Monaco, run by a family in which the son, Elliot Tiber, called us when he saw that the festival at Wallkill could not happen. He said that he had a permit for a festival but for chamber music. We went there and told him that the space in front of the motel was insufficient for what we had in mind. He was the one that brought me to Max Yasgur. We lost Wallkill on July 14, and on the 15th, I met Max Yasgur. He agreed to let us use his farm land. The miracle of Bethel, a coincidence for us, was salvaged in one day, and the press started to follow our every move." After overcoming the Wallkill

Opposite: One of the original festival posters, before the schedule was completely clear. Names of bands appear that, in reality, don't play shows, such as the Jeff Beck Group.

WOODSTOCK
MUSIC & ART FAIR
PRESENTS AN
AQUARIAN EXPOSITION
IN WHITE LAKE, N. Y.

Jimi Hendrix

Grateful Dead

Janis Joplin

★ ★ ★

3 Days of Peace & Music
AUGUST 1969

★ ★ ★

Friday 15th	Saturday 16th	Sunday 17th
Joan Baez	Canned Heat	The Band
Arlo Guthrie	Creedence Clearwater	Jeff Beck Group
Richie Havens	Grateful Dead	Blood, Sweat & Tears
Sly and The Family Stone	Janis Joplin	Joe Cocker
Tim Hardin	Jefferson Airplane	Crosby Stills & Nash
Nick Benes	Santana	Jimi Hendrix
Sweetwater	The Who	Iron Butterfly
	Jack Harrison	Ten Years After
		Jonny Winter

★ ★ ★ ★ ★ ★

HUNDREDS OF ACRES TO ROAM ON
Ticket Prices, One Day $7.00
Two Days $13.00, Three Days $18.00

obstacle, there was only a month left to put everything in motion for the festival. "We moved in a hurry. We had all of the materials and a good part of the contracts signed. We rushed to Bethel and started working by organizing different areas, chopping down trees in the areas that we needed free, and creating entry streets. I remember that I was desperately trying to install a telephone line in the concert area, in the middle of nowhere." The days of "information highways" were far away. Mobile phones and Internet did not exist, and communicating was much more complicated. "Oh, one could go crazy! You had to go all over the place to talk to someone, so we used walkie-talkies a lot and one lucky telephone line. We were in a big empty field at Bethel and we had to build everything. No one had ever done something like this; only the military during the war. We had to learn everything. We had to study ways to be able to bring 200,000 people to Woodstock; understand what to do about food, bathrooms, water, and trash. Then the technical part: the electricity, lights, water, and the sound system. In a month's time, we were doing what would have taken four months to do. There were 300 of us and we were working twenty-four hours a day." The people of Bethel were not very welcoming. "It was a small place, and that group of Beatniks that had invaded the area causing festival chaos was disliked by all."

Right: A group of young people from the organization involved in the festival area arrangement.

Left: Michael Lang drives a tractor on Max Yasgur's farm field in Bethel, in the space destined for the festival grounds.

Above: Michael Lang and other key players from the organization discuss the preparations for the festival.

Above: These are the cumulative tickets that permitted them to have access to all three days of the festival. In presale, the ticket cost six dollars per day, while it cost two dollars more to purchase it the day of. Eight-dollar tickets were almost unsold after the festival became a free event.

In any case, through the obstacles, creative solutions, and the technical support from anyone that had the slightest concept necessary, the week of the festival arrived. There were already 50,000 people in the area on Tuesday, and about 130,000 tickets were sold in advance. The promoters knew the crowd could grow up to 200,000. The festival was talked about a lot, and there were great expectations for it. "The Hog Farm youngsters, a hippie community led by Wavy Gravy, came to give us a hand. I met them in New York. I contacted them and asked them to come give a hand at the festival; run security the camp area, and they even started to organize a kitchen to coordinate meals. In many cases, we worked without the necessary permits. To not get arrested, I passed off as someone from the Hog Farm. There wasn't much difference between me and them..."

There were even talks with Abbie Hoffman's yippes, the politicized wing of the counterculture. "In reality, we had a lot of discussions with the whole underground world of the time because some thought that the festival wasn't an expression of counterculture, but a business deal. In reality, none of us had thought of an operation like this. Joel and John had invested their money. I thought it was right for them not to lose money, but rather we all make money from the festival since Artie and I worked a lot. There was nothing wrong with this. Of course, it was an investment. We had Roberts and Rosenman with the beginning capital, and Artie Kornfield who came from the music industry and organized the event, concerts, and festival. It was an opportunity. We wanted to organize the best festival possible but based off of different grounds. We wanted an event that reflected the ideas of the young." On paper, it was a bargain: the expected expenses were around $200,000, and with a ticket sold at six dollars, if 75,000 people came, then they all would have made money.

Left: Entrance tickets for a single day of the Woodstock festival.

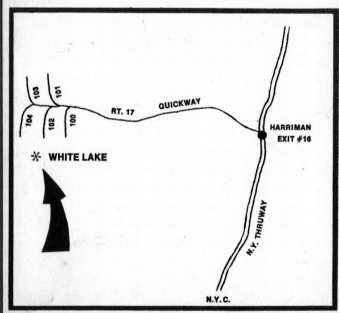

MOTELS ARE AVAILABLE IN SULLIVAN COUNTY AND VICINITY. FURTHER INFORMATION WILL BE AVAILABLE. PLEASE CHECK YOUR LOCAL NEWS MEDIA.

DIRECTIONS FROM BOSTON, MASS.
Take Massachusetts Turnpike to New York State Thruway—go South on Thruway to Exit 16 at Harriman, New York.

DIRECTIONS FROM PHILADELPHIA, PENN.
Take New Jersey Turnpike to Rt. 17 or New York State Thruway to Exit 16 North to Rt. 17 Quickway.

DIRECTIONS FROM NEW YORK
New York State Thruway to Exit 16, then take Rt. 17 Quickway to Exit 104. Proceed South for five miles.

(WITHIN 30 MILES OF FESTIVAL SITE TUNE TO WVOS 95.9 FM OR 1240 AM.)

WATCH FOR ROAD SIGNS TO PARKING AREA.
THERE WILL BE BUSSING FROM PARKING LOTS TO SITE.

WOODSTOCK MUSIC & ART FAIR
presents
AN AQUARIAN EXPOSITION
in
WHITE LAKE, N.Y.*

3 DAYS of PEACE & MUSIC

WITH

Joan Baez
Arlo Guthrie
Tim Hardin
Richie Havens
Incredible String Band
Ravi Shankar
Sly And The Family Stone
Bert Sommer
Sweetwater

Keef Hartley
Canned Heat
Creedence Clearwater
Grateful Dead
Janis Joplin
Jefferson Airplane
Mountain
Quill
Santana
The Who

The Band
Jeff Beck Group
Blood, Sweat and Tears
Joe Cocker
Crosby, Stills and Nash
Jimi Hendrix
Iron Butterfly
Ten Years After
Johnny Winter

FRI. AUG. 15   **SAT. AUG. 16**   **SUN. AUG. 17**

All programs subject to change without notice
*White Lake, Town of Bethel, Sullivan County, N.Y.

Above: The pages of the brochure that presented the festival and allowed for ticket reservations, filling out a specific form. **Opposite:** Other than the schedule, alternate activities to music and the details to reach the campgrounds were provided.

ART SHOW

Paintings and sculptures on trees, on grass, surrounded by the Hudson valley, will be displayed. Would be artists, ghetto artists, and accomplished artists will be glad to discuss their work, or the unspoiled splendor of the surroundings, or anything else that might be on your mind. If you're an artist, and you want to display, write for information.

CRAFTS BAZAAR

If you like creative knickknacks and old junk you'll love roaming around our bazaar. You'll see imaginative leather, ceramic, bead, and silver creations, as well as Zodiac Charts, camp clothes, and worn out shoes.

WORK SHOPS

If you like playing with beads, or improvising on a guitar, or writing poetry, or molding clay, stop by one of our work shops and see what you can give and take.

FOOD

There will be cokes and hotdogs and dozens of curious food and fruit combinations to experiment with.

HUNDREDS OF ACRES TO ROAM ON

Walk around for three days without seeing a skyscraper or a traffic light. Fly a kite, sun yourself. Cook your own food and breathe unspoiled air. Camp out: water and restrooms will be supplied. Tents and camping equipment will be available at the Camp Store.

MUSIC STARTS AT 4:00 P.M. ON FRIDAY, AND AT 1:00 P.M. ON SATURDAY AND SUNDAY.

It'll run for 12 continuous hours, except for a few short breaks to allow the performers to catch their breath.

(Gates open 10 A. M.)

Please Print

Send me _____ tickets for Fri., Aug. 15, at $7.00 each

Send me _____ tickets for Sat., Aug. 16, at $7.00 each

Send me _____ tickets for Sun., Aug. 17, at $7.00 each

Send me _____ 2 day tickets for Fri. & Sat., Aug. 15, 16, at $13.00 each

Send me _____ 2 day tickets for Sat. & Sun., Aug. 16, 17, at $13.00 ea.

Send me _____ Complete 3 day tickets for Fri., Sat., Sun., Aug. 15, 16, 17, at $18.00 each

Name_____

Address_____

City_____

State_____ Zip_____

Be sure to enclose a self-addressed, stamped envelope, with your check or money order (no cash please) payable to:
WOODSTOCK MUSIC, P. O. BOX 996
RADIO CITY STATION, NEW YORK 10019

"As soon as news started to spread about the festival, everyone started asking for more money. The move from Wallkill cost even more and little by little, the count was going out of control." Ultimately, the festival became a free event. "We had to have priorities. People entered without a ticket from the beginning. We didn't have time to build all the fences. When we saw how many people came and how many were coming, the priority was no longer tickets but food, water, that the music didn't stop, and that the people were happy. I think a huge part of our success was determined by this way of thinking. I had participated in many concerts where there was violence, especially with people that expected to enter without a ticket. We wanted everyone that participated to feel welcome. Originally, we had planned some box offices for the tickets but we also had free food, stages where anyone could perform, and free camping. We also had the fundamental collaboration of the Hog Farm that helped young kids in the city to be in a completely different situation. We only avoided those stupid confrontations that stupid rules can create. I knew from the beginning that the youngsters would have

Right: Photographer Baron Wolman from *Rolling Stone* magazine participates in the festival and takes various pictures like these, that catch a calm moment backstage at the event.

come without money or tickets. I also knew from the beginning that there wasn't a system that would have supported verifying hundreds of thousands of people, even if we wanted to.

"I thought of a different system: not allow the police to enter on the inside of the perimeter of the concert area, and make it so that everyone felt in some way responsible and dependent upon each other. In some way, all of this worked, also because it was a cultural and peaceful event, not a political event. Many

asked us for a space for a political intervention. One of those was Abbie Hoffman. Abbie called our offices one morning to tell us that if we didn't listen to him and the others about the yippie movement, there would be a big problem. We organized a meeting at East Village with Abbie and many others, a sort of conference. We agreed: they would occupy themselves in providing support to the youngsters, printing a 'survival guide' with useful advice, and they would have an assistance tent. We funded them with 10,000 dollars." At the

end, even Abbie Hoffman convinced himself that the festival was not like the others. He defined it as "Woodstock Nation."

The day of the festival came and the situation was totally chaotic because more than the expected number of people came. All of the entry streets to the festival were blocked.

You could only get there by foot and walking for many miles. Cars were parked everywhere, even in the middle of the street.

Above: In theory, the festival stage could have rotated in order to allow faster changes of scenes between one band and the next. In reality it didn't work due to the presence of many people on stage. The enormous weight of the Grateful Dead's sound system made it permanently inoperable.

"Backstage was different from all the others. Normally, bands arrived at the festivals, they would play and then leave. Instead, at Woodstock, many bands stayed for the entire weekend, since it was so hard to come back. The musicians stayed together also because the schedule was completely off and everyone was waiting for their turn. They played even at night. They didn't sleep, and stayed behind the stage. Incredible. The bands were closer to the audience, different than how they are today. They weren't stars, they weren't celebrities; they were deeply connected by counterculture and the movement. They reflected the wishes and dreams of the audience."

Many legends were born from negotiations with various artists involved with the festival. First of all, with the Rolling Stones and the Beatles. "We didn't call the Rolling Stones. All four of us agreed not to do it; they would have overshadowed the rest. It would have become their festival, and we did not like that. The Beatles didn't play anymore for a few years then, so we didn't even try. I tried to involve Lennon but had no luck. Dylan said no, Led Zeppelin said no, the Doors said no."

Woodstock had a much wider appeal, especially thanks to the extraordinary work of Michael Wadleigh, who transformed the festival into a worldwide event. "The film is still incredible today. Michael managed to not only transmit the event, but above all, the emotions from that day. It was a genuine film. For this reason, anyone who saw it at the theater truly was able to live in part the experience of the festival."

Lang himself admitted to having preferred some musical aspects of the festival compared to others. "I obviously loved all of the music played at the festival. I became fond of many; Richie Havens in particular, but also Country Joe McDonald, Crosby, Stills, & Nash. It was phenomenal having the opportunity to introduce a band like Santana to the whole world and let people hear how much passion Joe Cocker had. And the final set of Jimi Hendrix, with the 'Star-Spangled Banner'... although I have to tell the truth, the Sly and the Family Stone concert was more exciting for me. I have never in my life seen more intensity between the audience and a band."

Woodstock stayed in the collective imagination as the highest point of the hippie generation. What could follow that dream?

"I think that the ideas from then were still valid. I think that acting according to the simple rule 'peace and love' is essential to the human spirit. It was incredible that those there still play. They are still present in the minds of not only youngsters from the era but of many youth today," explained Lang.

Opposite: Jimi Hendrix and his band, the Experience, formed by drummer Mitch Mitchell (to the right), and bassist Noel Redding (seated).

THE HISTORY

Talking about Woodstock, an introduction is necessary: in spite of 500,000 eyewitnesses, there was no "defined" version of the festival facts. Everyone remembers it in their own way, as best as they can. We could—and we should—say that there were many Woodstock festivals, as many as the participants. What you are about to read is, for a long time, one of the many possible stories, although it's among the mainly validated. Before beginning the story of those three days, it is suitable to keep in mind the world of the most famous saying about Woodstock: "If someone tells you their memories about Woodstock, don't believe them. If they remember something about those three days, it means they weren't there."

We could say that the festival of Woodstock began on August 13 when the first avant-garde of the rock population came to the Bethel area, camping on Max Yasgur's farm.

Wednesday evening, tens of thousands of various people had already arrived, despite the fact that the structures weren't completed yet and the entrance fences were not up and running.

Left: While waiting in the long car line, two youngsters, sitting on their car, entertain themselves with a guitar. They were waiting for the long car line to move so they could reach the music festival.

Above: A boy smiles from the window of his Ford Mustang covered in peaceful writing, while on his way to the concert.

Opposite: On foot, by car, by means of good fortune. Young people crowd the streets around Bethel, trying to reach the festival area where they will engage in three days of "peace and music."

People came into the area without having anyone who was actually in charge of checking tickets, but all was calm.

The organizers expected between 150,000 and 200,000 people but the structure that they were finishing putting together could have accommodated maybe only a little more than 100,000.

These were the days when word-of-mouth facilitated the excitement of the event. The announced cast was certainly of great acclaim, but the motivating factor for many young people was the idea behind the festival itself, the possibility to be immersed in a completely different environment, on the farm, camping, living three days in absolute freedom, listening to music. There were never events like this, or at least on this scale, until then. The idea of participating in the festival greatly exceeded the attraction of a simple musical set. Even if the list of musicians alone was expected to showcase the "music and art fair," it was truly rich: Joan Baez, Grateful Dead, Jefferson Airplane, Joe Cocker, Country Joe McDonald, Richie Havens, Crosby, Stills, Nash & Young, Santana, the Who, The Band, Ten Years After, Sha Na Na, John Sebastian, Melanie, Blood Sweat & Tears, Johnny Winter, Tim Hardin, Canned Heat, Jeff Beck, Arlo Guthrie, Ravi Shankar, Sly and the Family Stone, the Incredible String Band, Creedence Clearwater Revival, Mountain, Bert Somer, Jimi Hendrix, Janis Joplin, Wavy Gravy, Keef Hartley Band, Sweetwater, Quill, and Paul Butterfield Blues Band.

Right: The traffic in the festival area blocked all of the entry streets for many miles. The concertgoers tried to reach Max Yasgur's farm by any form of transportation possible.

There were more than 100,000 people that arrived in Bethel by Thursday. Given the absolute impossibility to check entries, people managed to enter without purchasing a ticket. This did nothing more than change the attraction of the event for tens of thousands of other young people. By Friday, the area was completely blocked. Entrances to Bethel were literally unapproachable. Many people abandoned their cars on the streets and walked until they reached the site, traveling as far as twenty miles by foot.

Opposite and above: Young hippies try to reach the Woodstock festival area in any way possible. For many, the only possibility was to travel the remaining miles by foot since cars blocked the entry streets. The images from the era bring back the atmosphere of this peaceful "invasion."

Above and opposite: Joy and happiness, even under difficult conditions, underscored the three days of the festival. Despite the presence of 500,000 people, no major accidents were reported.

Following pages: Bill Eppridge, one of the two photographers of "life at Woodstock," took a series of photographs that show the atmosphere of these days. In this photo, while waiting in the long car line to reach the festival, a boy sleeps leaning between two cars.

Below: Many groups of young people use the school buses, transformed into campers, to reach the festival, and also for shelter at night.

Right: The Hog Farm was one of the historical hippie communes of the era. Mothers and children are shown here on the Hog Farm bus that was present at the festival. The members of the commune offered constant support to the organization and to the young concertgoers.

First Day

The first day of the festival was chaotic. Since it was impossible to reach the concert area, the bands that were scheduled to perform first could not get there in time. So all of Friday morning passed by without anyone playing a single musical note.

In order to get things in order, the organizers had to deal with many overlooked details. There weren't enough bathrooms, the food and water were already

Below: A view of the half-a-million people who came together from all over the country to celebrate the three days of the Woodstock festival.

running out, the stage was not finished, and the electric cables weren't even in position. The only transportation available to quickly reach the festival was a helicopter that was used by the organizers to help the artists get to the stage area. The delay was only an hour but Michael Lang couldn't find the artists who were supposed to perform first: Sweetwater. He asked musician Tim Hardin to fill in, who refused. The job of opening the concert fell back on Richie Havens's shoulders. The black folksinger, one of the few African Americans in a musical environment substantially dominated by whites, made his debut in 1961 on the popular scene of Greenwich Village in New York. He received outstanding interest from the audience for his talent as a singer, and especially for his intense rhythmic guitar style.

Havens didn't write many songs; he loved to be an interpreter, so this allowed him to develop a diverse skillset. His real success came on the Woodstock stage where he performed first. Havens went on stage, accompanied by two other musicians: Daniel Ben Zebulon on drums and Paul "Deano" Wilson on guitar.

According to the most accredited versions, Havens began playing at 5:05 P.M., greeted by a thunderous applause from the audience that was waiting with great anticipation. The set was composed of around ten songs, according to many sources, which contradicts what Havens stated afterward: he claimed to have played for around three hours.

In any case, it was truly an extraordinary and intense performance. Havens and his bandmates mixed songs from traditional folk and blues with rock, including "From the Prison," "Get Together," "Minstrel from Gault," "I'm a Stranger Here," "High Flying Bird," and "I Can't Make It Anymore." He was the first to sing a Beatles song, "With a Little Help from My Friends" (also sung again later by Joe Cocker), followed by "Handsome Johnny." Havens returned to the stage more times to play an encore demanded by the audience. After having improvised a Beatles medley with "Strawberry Fields Forever" and "Hey Jude," he came back for a new improvisation. He started playing the old spiritual "Motherless Child," but transformed it into the new song, "Freedom." As viewers can see from Michael Wadleigh's 1970 film *Woodstock*, Havens reached the climax of his performance in a sort of rhythmic trance that was absolutely captivating.

Richie Havens

Above: Spectators climb on the scaffolding that was built to support the amplifiers so they could hear Richie Havens's performance.

Opposite: Richie Havens opens the Woodstock festival on August 15, 1969.

74

Left and above: The area around the stage was so crowded that some young people climbed on the scaffolding and the support structures to get a better view.

The festival did not begin with a lucky performance like it seemed, but with a magical performance by a remarkable artist that set the tone for the entire event. "Freedom," sang Havens, mixing the invocation to the text of the traditional song: "Sometimes I feel like a son without a mother, far away, far away from home." His musical expression captured the general feeling of the audience, as thousands of people were "disoriented," away from their home towns, families, principles, or rules.

Left and above: Some couples relaxing on Max Yasgur's farmland during the festival. In those three days during Woodstock, there were two births.

Following pages: A young hippie couple sitting on the grass at the farm where the festival took place. Today, it has been transformed into a museum dedicated to the event.

Left: A girl looks at the photographer's lens. The pass attached to her pants identifies her as a performer.

They were like motherless children of an America that didn't acknowledge them, and they asked for freedom. After Woodstock—and especially after the film came out—Havens became an international star yet he remained true to himself throughout his whole life. He published albums full of beautiful songs interpreted with great intensity and "devoted" passages. These represented the "silver lining" of his whole career, which favored a commitment to peaceful, ecological, and societal resolutions, from his debut in the early sixties until his death in 2013.

Above: A picture of the camping area designated for tents in the area surrounding the festival. Soon, the rain would make the ground particularly difficult for camping.

Left: A group of young people build a structure thrown together with wood during the days before the festival began. Several hippie communities coming from every area of the United States arrived at the festival with the intention of selling artisan products, but also to contribute to the success of the event.

Following pages: Young people sitting on the roof of a school bus painted with "flower power."

Left: This panoramic view of the festival area highlights the half a million people crowded in front of the stage and in the large camping area behind it.

In order to establish a stronger spiritual connection between the participants, and to remind everyone that the festival was a gathering born under the sign of peace and love, the organizers decided to call upon a guru who, in these days, was gaining a lot of interest in the United States: Sri Swami Satchidananda. Only a few months before, he led an event at Carnegie Hall in New York City. He also arrived late to Woodstock due to the congestion and went on stage after Havens to bless the crowd with these words: "I am overwhelmed with joy to see the entire youth of America gathered here in the name of the fine art of music . . . In fact, through the music, we can work wonders. Music is a celestial sound and it is the sound that controls the whole universe, not atomic vibrations. Sound energy, sound power, is much, much greater than any other power in this world. And one thing I would very much wish you all to remember is that with sound, we can make—and at the same time, break. Even in the war-field, to make the tender heart an animal, sound is used. Without that war band, that terrific sound, man will not become animal to kill his own brethren.

"So that proves that you can break with sound, and if we care, we can make also.

"So I am very happy to see that we are all here gathered to create some sounds—to find that peace and joy through the celestial music. And I am really very much honored for having been given this opportunity of opening this great, great music festival. I should have come a little earlier to do that job, but as you all know, thousands of brothers and sisters are on the way and it's not that easy to reach here. America leads the whole world in several ways. Very recently, when I was in the East, the grandson of Mahatma Gandhi met me and asked me what's happening in America, and I said 'America is becoming whole. America is helping everybody in the material field, but the time has come for America to help the whole world with spirituality also.' And that's why from the length and breadth, we see people—thousands of people, yoga-minded, spiritual-minded. The whole of last month I was in Hawaii and I was on the West Coast and witnessed it again. So let all our actions, and all our arts, express yoga.

Swami Satchidananda

Opposite: A photo of Swami Satchidananda, the guru who gave a brief speech to the young people at the festival. "Sound energy, sound power, is much, much greater than any other power in this world."

"Through the sacred art of music, let us find peace that will pervade all over the globe. Often we hear groups of people shouting, 'Fight for peace.' I still don't understand how they are going to fight and then find peace. Therefore, let us not fight for peace, but let us find peace within ourselves first. And the future of the whole world is in your hands. You can make or break. But you are really here to make the world and not to break it. I am seeing it. There is a dynamic manpower here. The hearts are meeting. Just yesterday I was in Princeton, at Stony Brook in a monastery, where about two hundred or three hundred Catholic monks and nuns met and they asked me to talk to them under the heading of 'East and West—One Heart.' Here, I really wonder whether I am in the East or West. If these pictures or the films are going to be shown in India, they would certainly never believe that this is taken in America. For here, the East has come into the West. And with all my heart, I wish a great, great success in this music festival to pave the way for many more festivals in many other parts of this country. But the entire success is in your hands, not in the hands of a few organizers. Naturally, they have come forward to do some job. I met them. I admire them. But still, in your hands the success lies. The entire world is going to watch this. The entire world is going to know what the youth of America can do for humanity. So, every one of you should be responsible for the success of this festival."

At the end of his speech, the crowd joined Sri Swami Satchidananda in singing the popular Hindu mantra, "Hari Om, Rama Rama."

Above: A group of young mothers sit in the crowd at the festival with their children. The traditional concept of family was extensively discussed by hippies.

The situation behind the stage was growing worse instead of getting better. The extreme street congestion was out of control at this point, and the artists arrived with extreme difficulty. Sweetwater, who was supposed to open the day, finally arrived and managed to make it to the stage. The band—already well-known in the psychedelic rock network of Los Angeles, and who had performed with the Doors and the Animals during their tour—went on stage a little after 6:00 P.M.

Left: A little girl is filmed by one of Michael Wadleigh's film crew. The film *Woodstock* won an Academy Award for Best Documentary Feature in 1970.

Above: One of the members of the Merry Pranksters in front of the legendary bus, "Further," with some children from Ken Kesey's commune.

Above: A boy standing up in the crowd with a sign that reads, "Love your animal friends, don't ea͏
ͣhem." Animal rights and environmentalism are among the legacies of the hippie era.

Right: A cameraman at his aerial post above the crowd's heads. The film made Woodstock known to the world.

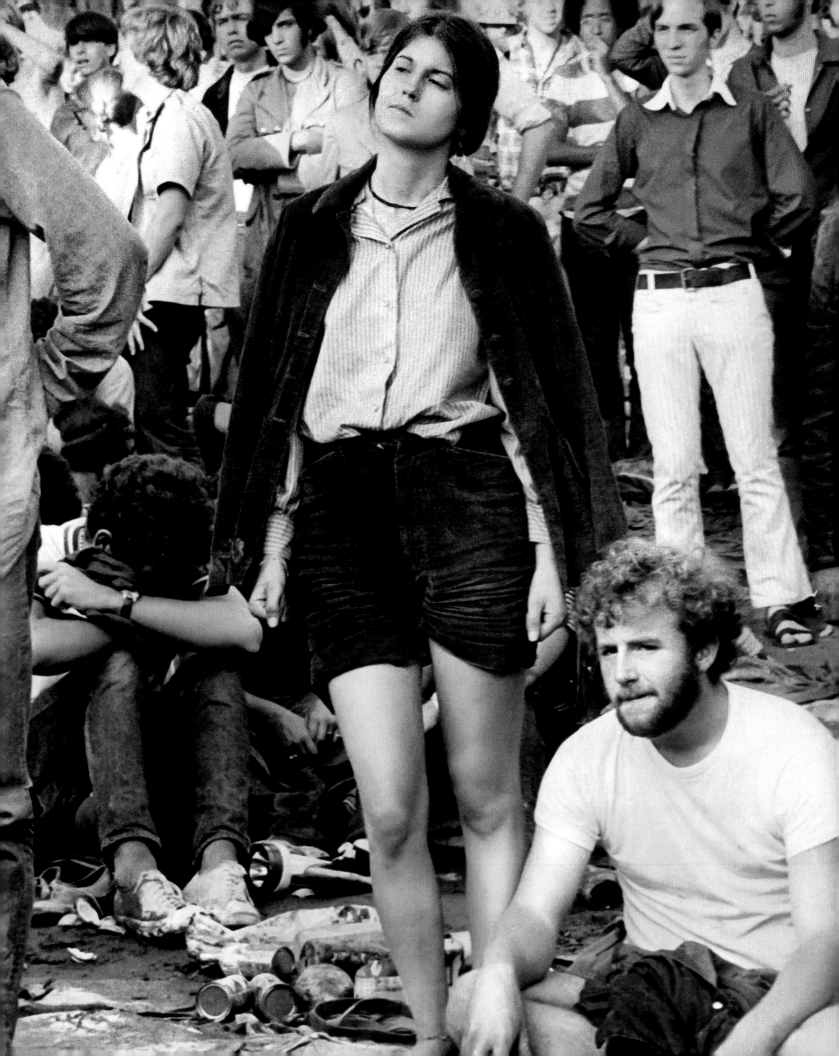

Left: The young girls with the hippie style were certainly big protagonists of the event. Their presence at the concert became a symbol for the movement of female liberation, which, in those years, was declared as a movement of public opinion, and it reached significant achievements.

Above: A completely naked girl attending the concert dances in the audience. This is one of the strongest images of sexual freedom that the young generation was so desperate for.

Havens had concluded his performance with a version of "Motherless Child," and Sweetwater opened their set with the same song, interpreting it in a completely different way. With only a few minutes between one performance and the next, the crowd somehow had a perfect grasp of what this represented at that time: rock—not a genre, not a style, but a way to confront music that did not conform to the rules. It was a movement toward sharing, expressive freedom, emotion, the desire to change, and to connect the change with both the heart and mind. For Sweetwater, it certainly was not one of their best performances, but band members Nancy Nevins, Alex Del Zoppo, Fred Herrera, August Burns, Alan Malarowitz, Elpidio "Pete" Cobian, and Albert Moore put on a forty-five-minute set onstage that was perfect to enliven the festival crowd. They played nine songs and ended the performance with "Let the Sunshine In" and "Oh Happy Day" amid much audience applause.

Then it was Bert Sommer's turn. Even if his name is unknown today, his hair was seen for many years by millions of people all over the world. In fact, it was drawn on the original poster of one of the most celebrated and revolutionary musicals of the time, *Hair* in which Sommer was one of the characters.

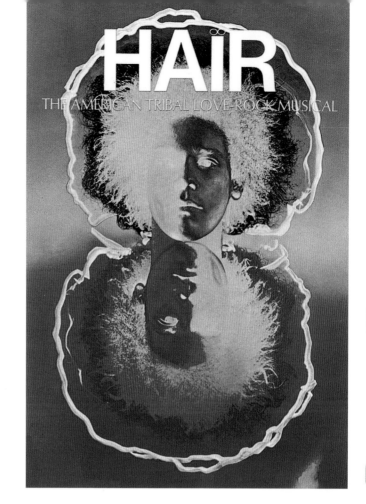

Sommer was one of the artists that Artie Kornfield had bet on from the beginning. He had followed him since the beginning of his career and would produce several of his albums.

The song choices for the festival were balanced by songs taken from his debut album and new ones that Sommer wanted to promote. He came to Woodstock together with two other musicians, Charlie Bilello and Ira Stone. He went on stage in bare feet, flared pants, and headband in his hair, around 7:00 P.M.

Opposite: A couple dance to the rhythm of the music, standing among the young concertgoers.

Above: The poster for *Hair*, the first hippie musical that arrived on the Broadway stage of 1968, showcases the image of Bert Sommer with his iconic hair.

Above: An exhausted girl sleeps on the hay bales in an area of Max Yasgur's farm during one of the intermissions.

Above: A boy with long hair holds a guitar while sitting down on an aerial platform built in a tree, seeking shelter from the mud that invaded the area.

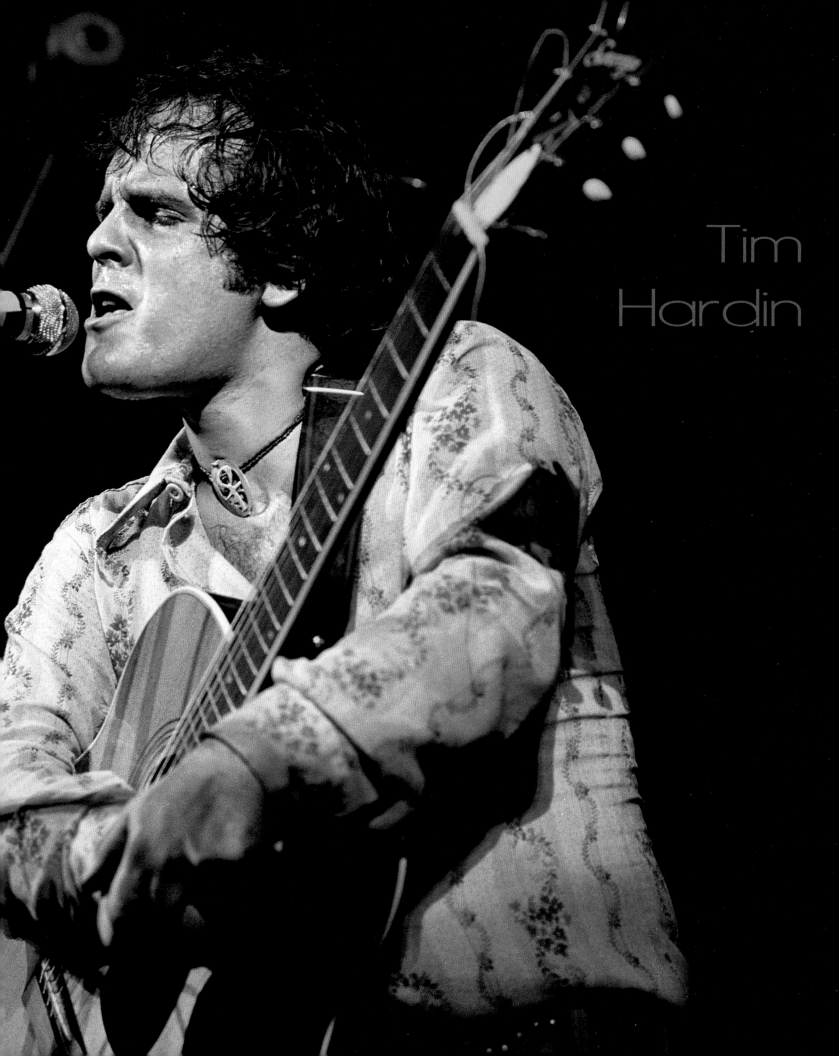

Tim
Hardin

"Jennifer," followed by "The Road to Travel," "I Wondered Where You'd Be," "She's Gone," "Things Are Going My Way," "And When It's Over," "Jeanette," then "A Note that Read" and "Smile"—a perfect set for the sunset and for creating an atmosphere of peace and love. It was yet another "generational" song to arouse enthusiasm. It was their beautiful version of "America," a song originally written by Simon & Garfunkel, that received the first standing ovation at the festival, with an enthusiastic crowd applauding Sommer and his bandmates.

For many unknown artists of the time period, the Woodstock festival opened the door to international fame. For Sommer, things went differently. After Woodstock, the American artist wasn't particularly successful. This made him very bitter because his excellent performance—considered by many the best of the first day of the festival—was not included on either the record or in the documentary of the event.

The first artist to perform as the evening approached—and the last to go on stage before the rain—was Tim Hardin. Lang had asked the artist to perform at the beginning of the day, but Hardin, thanks to a heroin dose, wasn't able to do it. Many different stories circulated about what happened. The first, and most accredited, is the one according to Hardin. Already a drug addict for some time, he was anxious after having seen the enormous crowd. He took drugs to calm down and only went on stage when his physical and emotional conditions returned to normal. Hardin had already had some success behind him, especially "Reason to Believe," a song included in his 1966 debut album. He also grew up in New York's Greenwich Village and built moderate fame as a singer-songwriter, thanks to a single success, the beautiful "If I Were a Carpenter," and also producing several albums. However, he never managed to achieve huge success, partly because his addiction influenced him and his fear of the stage often kept him away from concerts. Hardin played a solo song and then another nine with a band formed by Richard Bock, Steve Booker, Giles Malkine, Bill Chelf, and the young Glen Moore and Ralph Towner, who shortly afterward would form the group Oregon. Hardin performed admirably and his performance was welcomed with enthusiasm. He offered a rich and sophisticated musical performance to the audience that was in line with the singer-songwriter style.

Opposite: A picture from Tim Hardin's performance. He began singing when it was already dark. At the end of his performance, it started raining.

The playlist of songs performed by Hardin was as follows: "How Can We Hang on to a Dream," "Susan," "If I Were a Carpenter," "Reason to Believe," "You Upset the Grace of Living When You Lie," "Speak Like a Child," "Snow White Lady," "Blues on My Ceiling," "Simple Song of Freedom," and "Misty Roses." Even if Hardin did not have the satisfaction of seeing his songs included on the *Woodstock* album and film, this didn't stop him from being successful until his death in 1980.

The teachings from India came to Woodstock. Only a year earlier in 1968, the Beatles had opened the door to Asia, when they visited Maharishi Mahesh during the month of February. George Harrison had introduced the sitar and Indian music to the Beatles world and to Western culture, while the Byrds and the Rolling Stones had contributed to the spread of Indian music. Harrison had taken sitar lessons from one of the most reknowned Indian artists, Ravi Shankar, whose fame grew little by little in the States, especially among the younger generation. Shankar had already performed two years before at the Monterey festival, achieving great success, and the organizers invited him to also perform at Woodstock. The rain had already begun to fall when Shankar went on stage with Ustad Alla Rakha and Maya Kulkarni, transforming the festival into wonderful magic. They performed three songs: "Raga Puriya-Dhanashri," the incredibly captivating "Tabla Solo in Jhaptal" by Alla Rakha, and the conclusion, "Raga Manj Kmahaj." It was twenty-one minutes in when the interaction between Shankar and Rakha touched high peaks, with a slow beginning and a crescendo that pushed both musicians to improvise.

Ravi Shankar

Above: Alla Rakha on the tabla and Ravi Shankar on the sitar during their performance. The Indian musician became well-known after performing The Concert for Bangladesh, a benefit concert organized by George Harrison in 1971.

American singer-songwriter Melanie's Woodstock performance was also highly applauded. Although relatively unknown at the time, the artist was invited to perform on stage, thanks to a twist of fate. The young twenty-two-year-old had recently released her debut album, which contained a hit song destined to become a big success: "Beautiful People." Her record company's offices, Buddha Records, were in the same building as Woodstock Ventures. Melanie, as soon as she heard that Lang and the others were organizing a festival, knocked on their door and asked to participate in the event. When she obtained approval, on August 15, she headed toward Bethel, accompanied by her mother. However, like everyone else, they were blocked.

The two women reached the El Monaco hotel where they found other musicians, like Janis Joplin, waiting to reach the concert location. A helicopter arrived to get Melanie to take her to her destination. She was forced to leave her mom on the ground. At this point, a story intervenes that is worth telling, even if it might not be true. The best re-creation of the facts says that Melanie was in the audience singing and playing her guitar, and she provoked such enthusiasm that the organizers were forced to call her backstage. A second version, less romantic but not less

Melanie

Left: A moment during Melanie Safka's performance, a little before midnight on August 15.

Opposite: Arlo Guthrie, singer-songwriter and son of legendary folksinger Woody Guthrie, on the Woodstock stage.

entertaining, says that Melanie was forced to convince the security crew to let her go backstage with them singing her "Beautiful People." Whatever the truth was, it is certain that Melanie was backstage at the same time the Scottish group Incredible String Band refused to go on stage because of the rain.

Since the young artist was available to perform, her turn came, greeted by thousands of flames lit by the audience, at the invitation of the announcer: "You are the biggest crowd ever gathered at a concert, it's dark, you can't imagine how many of you there are. Light some matches and look who you have next to you." The test worked and Melanie was overwhelmed by emotion, as one can understand listening to the performance recording again. The artist expressed these feelings in a beautiful song, "Lay Down (Candles in the Rain)" that became one of her biggest successes. Melanie went on stage alone around 11:00 P.M. and presented seven songs to the crowd: "Close to It All," "Momma Momma," "Beautiful People," "Animal Crackers," a cover of "Mr. Tambourine Man" by Bob Dylan, "Tuning My Guitar," and "Birthday of the Sun."

Just before midnight, Arlo Guthrie took the stage. The singer-songwriter and son of legendary Woody Guthrie was already well-known, not only because of his father, but also for having brought success to a song that was a pungent satire against the war and against American society. "Alice's Restaurant Massacree"—more well known as "Alice's Restaurant"—was included in Guthrie's debut album in 1967. Guthrie performed in a

quartet that was comprised of Bob Arkin, John Pilla, and Paul Motian, one of the best drummers in the history of jazz. The set lasted about fifty minutes and was opened by the beautiful song "Coming into Los Angeles," followed by "Wheel of Fortune," "Walking Down the Line" (a talking blues in which there was a parallel between the Exodus and the violence at Berkeley University in California), "Oh Mary Don't You Weep," "Every Hand in the Land," and then finally ended with the hymn "Amazing Grace."

A few days after the festival, the movie that director Arthur Penn made based on the story of "Alice's Restaurant," was released in movie theaters. Guthrie's well-deserved success and popularity grew enormously, as the world recognized his talent.

Joan Baez closed out the long, first day of the Woodstock festival. At that time, she was five months pregnant and went on stage a little before one in the morning. Baez was a real celebrity for the festival audience. She was Bob Dylan's muse and lover at the height of Greenwich Village's popularity, and she was one of the prominent personalities during the American folk revival, as well as an activist of the peace movement. In fact, while she was on the Woodstock stage, her husband, David Harris, was in prison for refusing the call from the army to go to the Vietnam War, and she herself had marched at the side of Martin Luther King. Joan was a real star of "new" music, having performed on stage already for a decade with current successful albums. She kept her folksy roots, but for some time was tied to the world of rock. Her set was the longest of the day, opened by "Oh Happy Day" and followed by thirteen other songs, many performed solo with her guitar, including, "The Last Thing on My Mind," a cover of "I Shall Be Released" by Bob Dylan, "No Expectation," the wonderful "Joe Hill" (dedicated to the figure that is considered one of the fathers of the U.S. union movement), then "Sweet Sir Galahad," "Hickory Wind," a cover of the Byrds' "Drugstore Truck Driving Man" (accompanied by Jeffrey Shurtleff and Richard Festinger), "I Live One Day at a Time," "Take Me Back to the Sweet Sunny South," and "Let Me Wrap You in My Warm and Tender Love." Then came the grand finale with an emotional a cappella version of "Swing Low Sweet Chariot" and "We Shall Overcome," which became an anthem for the civil rights movement.

Right: The performance by Joan Baez was among the favorites during the first day of the festival. The singer was nicknamed "the nightingale of Woodstock" after her performance.

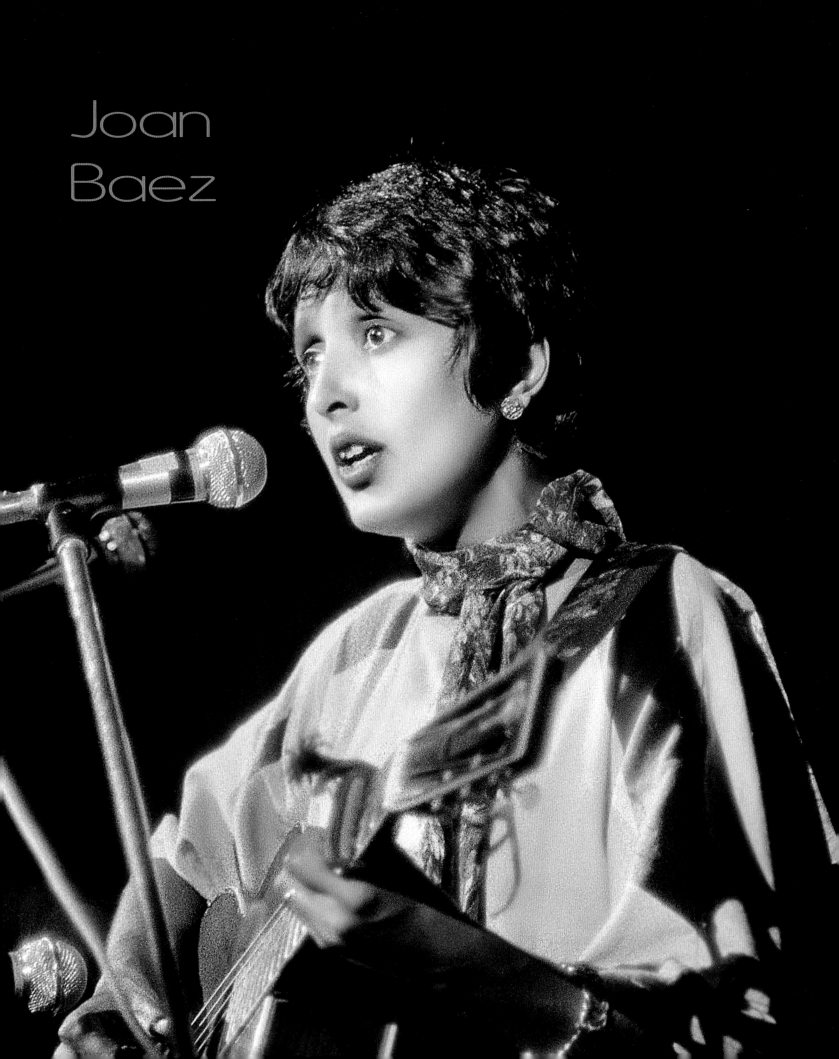

Joan
Baez

Left: Some young people get completely soaked from the heavy rain during the first big downpour at Woodstock.

At the end of Joan Baez's performance, the weather suddenly changed. The light drizzle turned into a pouring rain that forced the audience to look for shelter anywhere possible, creating truly difficult conditions for their first festival night. The weather was no doubt far worse than originally forecast. According to some, the rain that fell that weekend surpassed the seasonal average. Hundreds of thousands of young people had arrived in the area, with just as many still blocked on the road, and who were already preparing to go back because it was no longer possible to reach Bethel. Almost none of them had paid the entrance fee. The four organizers from Woodstock Ventures took action and decided to declare that the festival be free: "It is a free concert from now on. That doesn't mean that anything goes; it means that we are putting free music on stage. It means that those that organized this festival, who put up the money for it, are going to take a bit of a bath, a big bath. It's not hype, they will get hurt. What that means is that these people think that your welfare and music is damn more important than dollars. Now, the most important thing that you have to remember tonight, whether you go to sleep in the woods or stay right here, is that the person near you is your brother. And you damn well better treat each other that way because if you don't, then we blow the whole thing. But we've got it, right there."

The following morning, even to optimistic people, it was clear that the situation was difficult. The organizers needed to find food and water for hundreds of thousands of people, the toilets would never suffice, and the rain had reduced the area to mud. The community that could have guaranteed supplies, Food for Love, was not able to offer help to everyone. It was not easy for Lang and his group to find a supplier for the festival; the major companies refused the original invitation from Woodstock Ventures, especially because no one before then had to feed so many people, and no one felt they were able to do it. Nathan's Hot Dogs backed down because it couldn't make an agreement on cost with the organizers, but especially because it didn't like the move to Bethel. They accepted Food for Love, a community run by three young people without particular experience. They were Charles Baxter, Jeffrey Joerger, and Lee Howard. Woodstock Ventures didn't have a better alternative two weeks before the beginning of the festival. Even if they would have had the requisite experience, the situation wouldn't have been much better. Already, by the end of the first day, the food brought by Food for Love was almost gone, and many of the stands were not even set up properly to sell it. Thanks to the blocked roads, the supplies could not be delivered. Woodstock Ventures had thought of having a token system, or a voucher, to avoid the use of money inside the festival area, but it only created complications given the enormous rush of people with cash on them and no place to supply tokens.

The festival participants endured the problems with patience. According to all of the witnesses, the spirit of sharing allowed them to move forward, even with the little they had. The lines at the stands became endless, just like those around the few available bathrooms. Somehow the atmosphere was generally positive, even when the weather became worse. The weather would sometimes clear up, and then begin raining cats and dogs again. Somebody arriving from Bethel sold sandwiches at higher prices than planned, beginning at 25 cents and then increasing prices all the way up to a dollar. On Saturday night, some infuriated attendees started attacking and destroying stands. To save the festival from a gigantic food disaster, many groups came to help. This included the people in charge of Monticello, Jewish Community Center, the people from St. Peter's Church, members from the Methodist church, members from a Presbyterian church, local citizens, and owners of local restaurants and cafes. At first, restaurateurs thought about being opportunistic, but given the situation, they simply offered a hand by preparing sandwiches. The most active and important organization was Hugh Romney's Hog Farm, known as Wavy Gravy. Lang had called Romney and his group to take on the role of setting up the festival security (the "Please Force," as Romney called it). The Hog Farm, one of the most well-known hippie communities on the East Coast, conducted various tasks.

Left: A girl smokes while sitting on a camping bed in one of the "release tents" assembled in the festival area, run by various organizations. These tents provided aid for the young concertgoers in case of sickness, especially for those who used drugs.

Above: One of the many stands built in the wooded area of Max Yasgur's farm, a sort of market for hippie products such as necklaces, incense, posters, and different types of objects. In this case, the objects include smoking paraphernalia.

The Farmers arrived a few days before the event to create paths that would make foot traffic easier in the area. They organized various fire pits to allow for contained fires. They also created a "free kitchen" to feed the crowd. Romney and his group became a part of history for having introduced cereal to the hippie culture; as it was less expensive and faster to cook, the crowd from the Hog Farm chose vegetables, brown rice, and granola as the main ingredients in their dishes. Romney went on stage Sunday morning, to defend those who suffered damage. He announced, "There is a man who sells hamburgers that saw his stand on fire last night. But he still has some things available. So those who still think that capitalism isn't so crazy could help him and buy some hamburgers." Outside of capitalism, there was the Hog Farm that prepared food for anyone, for free. "What we have in mind is to bring breakfast in bed to 400,000 people," Romney said from the stage. "It won't be bacon and steak but it will be good food and we are bringing it to you. There's no doubt that this is heaven, boys and girls, we are feeding each other." The Hog Farm managed to distribute thousands of bowls of cereal to the spectators, especially to those in the first rows that didn't move from their spot where they could see and hear the music so well. According to the Farmers, food actually never truly disappeared. Between their work together with the other organizations, including the army that threw packages of food to the crowd from helicopters, there was enough to eat—maybe not much, but there was some. And whoever managed to get it willingly shared it with others.

Right: One of the camp kitchens built by the Hog Farm members that distributed food for free to the young people at the festival. The Hog Farm managed to feed the overwhelming majority of the crowd, by serving cereal.

Left: The shortage of water was one of the biggest problems at the festival. Five trucks came daily to bring water. Instead, in this picture, you can see a truck distributing milk.

Above: People in line with paper plates in hand to get food from one of the camp kitchens managed by the Hog Farm.

Left: A couple relax during a break between sets. This time often ended up being used to recover and build up more strength.

Above: A couple with their little boy at Woodstock. There were many children that participated in the festival with their young parents and hippie families.

Other than the food and water supply problem, there was also the issue of cleanliness. Chip Monck—master of ceremonies at Woodstock, by request of Michael Lang—asked the crowd from the stage to clean up all that they could, and everywhere. According to Lang, the risk, given the difficult hygienic conditions, was that someone would come to block the festival, for fear of the spreading of infection. In the meantime, many doctors had arrived in the area to manage the first aid tent. There was a death in the morning. Raymond Mizak, a seventeen-year-old, was victim of an accident when a tractor passed over a sleeping bag that he was sleeping in. They helped him right away and brought him to a less congested area, but the helicopter that could have taken him to the nearest hospital arrived after the boy had died. On Sunday, another boy died: an eighteen-year-old who was an ex-soldier in Vietnam. The doctors who had their base in the garden at the back of Yasgur's house tried to help him, just like they had done for hundreds of other people, but they weren't so lucky this time. There were about fifty doctors working in the two first aid tents, where, according to calculations, about 5,000 people were cared for. Most had foot wounds (usually from having stepped on broken glass), many suffered bad acid trips, and still others suffered far worse problems. According to some sources, the doctors performed three tracheotomies and also took care of someone who slipped into a diabetic coma. As the story goes, two births were also recorded: the first in a car stuck in traffic, the second at the Monticello hospital following a helicopter flight. However, no one has ever stated that they were born at Woodstock, and there aren't official documents that prove it. Many instead claim they were conceived in those three days—and they may be right.

Left: The most famous couple of Woodstock, kept alive on the disc cover. Nick and Bobbi Ercoline were engaged for just a few weeks at that time. They are still married after fifty years.

Second Day

On Sunday morning, the combination of rain, chaos, a lack of food and water, overcrowded restrooms, a half million people at the festival and just as many in the streets around Bethel who were unable to reach the concert area, all created critical conditions. The state governor of New York, Nelson Rockefeller, was forced to send the National Guard to the festival—10,000 men to be exact. It would have been another destabilizing element, but the people in charge of Sullivan County convinced him to stop, temporarily declaring the area a "disaster zone," so they could put into practice a more rapid response unit to manage the complicated situation. Incredibly, it was the "spirit of Woodstock," however, that took the upper hand. The crowd began helping one another, offering each other a hand, and avoiding the worst.

The Quill opened the music event on Sunday. The band—made up of brothers Cole, Jon, and Dan, along with Roger North, Norman Rogers, and Phil Thayer— had put together rock, jazz, and psychedelic music in original and interesting arrangements, which had gained interest among the New England and New York clubs, but Woodstock was their first big performance. They played four songs in a little less than a half hour: "They Live the Life," "That's How I Eat," "Driftin'," and "Waitin' for You." During "Waitin' for You," the band tried to involve the crowd in an improvised jam session, by tossing percussion instruments to concertgoers in the first few rows. This had worked well in small clubs, creating enthusiasm, but with hundreds of thousands of people, this didn't particularly have an effect. Due to synchronization problems of the audio with the images, the Quill did not appear in the festival's documentary.

Completely improvised was the following performance by Country Joe McDonald and his band, Fish, who were scheduled for the following day. The Carlos Santana band was supposed to have gone on stage at that time, but the group was still assembling. The organizers needed to find someone to replace them. Country Joe McDonald, after a brief discussion with the organizers, agreed to go on, just to entertain the crowd. Someone passed him a guitar that didn't even have a strap, only a string to rest on his shoulders, and he began to sing.

Left: A guy wears his chair on his head with his hands behind his back, to protect himself from the rain that was covering the festival area.

Above: A couple rolled up in a blanket on the side of the stage.

Right: A couple hug on the high part of the natural dip where the festival was taking place.

The set was opened by "Janis," a song that Country Joe had written and dedicated to musician Janis Joplin. Then, solo with only a guitar and his voice, he performed "Donovan's Reef," "Heartaches by the Number," "Ring of Fire," "Tennessee Stud," "Rockin' Round the World," "Flying High," and "Seen a Rocket." The crowd didn't pay much attention; it was lunch time, and many were busy looking for something to eat. Others were simply thinking about something else. Nevertheless, Country Joe had his "ace in the hole" that had become his band's trademark, the popular "Fish Cheer," urging the crowd to help spell out "Fish" one letter at a time. "Gimme an F!" he demanded, ultimately spelling out "F-I-S-H." McDonald was one of the Californian musicians and pioneers who combined irony, protest, peace, and music. He was also one of the first to protest the Vietnam War, writing a song in 1965 titled, "I-Feel-Like-I'm-Fixin'-to-Die-Rag," later re-released in 1967, achieving great success. His commitment didn't stop there; he was active in the movement and was the first to outwardly show concern for veterans, asking the nation to treat them with respect and compassion. Country Joe wrote his song, nicknamed "Rag," in a half hour, with the explicit proposal to point fingers against the involvement of young people in the war, through conscription, using irony but also crude images, and openly talking about death. With the growing protests against the war, also believed to have polarized the song, it gave the title to the band's second album and became one of the highlights of their concerts. In the summer of 1968 during a concert in New York, the drummer of the band proposed that the group transform the yell, introducing the word "fuck"— something that the crowd particularly enjoyed.

Left: The audience attends a performance during the second day of the festival, while the rain creates a short break.

Left: Hugh Romney, also known as Wavy Gravy, one of the founders of the Hog Farm, addresses the crowd from the stage. Romney is still an entertainer and peace activist.

Emissaries from the *Ed Sullivan Show* previously had a different reaction when they went to see the band, and afterward banned them from their broadcasts forever.

At Woodstock, Country Joe McDonald decided to abandon the stage after singing his songs for about half an hour because only a few listened to him. Dissatisfied with the crowd's reaction, he eventually went back on stage and began the "Fuck Cheer," which concluded with asking, "What's that spell?" and the inevitable response from the audience, before starting to sing "I-Feel-Like-I'm-Fixin'-to-Die-Rag"—this time with full attention and enthusiasm from the people. McDonald managed to involve the audience even more. "Listen people, I don't know how you all think you can stop the war if you don't know how to sing better than this. There are about 300,000 assholes like you here; I want you to start singing!" The very loud "fuck you" screamed by hundreds of thousands of people immediately became the strongest chant of a generation that no longer wanted to go to war, and for Country Joe, it became a trademark, reinforced by the film throughout the world.

The messages read on stage during the three festival days were a constant occurrence. Internet and cell phones were still far away at this point, and the only way to get in contact with someone you lost, or try to find a lost object, or simply get help, was to send a note on stage. Chip Monck read the famous stage announcements in a timely fashion. They were even included on the festival albums.

Chip Monck is one of the figures with a well deserved, significant place in the history of rock, not only because he was a legendary stage and light designer but also for his role in the composition of "A Hard Rain's Gonna Fall" by Bob Dylan, who wrote the lyrics on his typewriter. He was also known for his work at the Village Gate Club in New York City in the early sixties, at the Newport festivals, at the Monterey festival of 1967, and at the one in Miami in 1968. It was in Miami where Monck got in contact with Lang, who would call him to design the Woodstock stage.

Much of the work ended up being wasted because of the move from Wallkill to Bethel. It made it impossible to assemble some of the structures and many of the lights, which ended up remaining disassembled under the stage. The festival audience however knew little about the designer's role, and instead knew him as "master of ceremonies," appointed to give announcements on stage—including the famous warnings on the danger of consuming brown acid. All of the small handwritten notes read by Monck that went up on stage, allowing the people to communicate with one another, were just as important as the warnings.

The history of Woodstock is full of little magical moments, incredible minutes where unexpected things happened. These are the moments that made the festival unique, that gave life to the legends of "Woodstock nation" and of the "three days of peace, love, and music," that kept the dream alive.

One of these moments was Max Yasgur's entrance

Left: In this group picture taken backstage at the festival, you can see the legendary Bill Graham in the center. He was the most important organizer of American concerts who emerged on the San Francisco scene in the middle of the sixties.

on stage. He was the owner of the farm where the festival was taking place. Yasgur went to Michael Lang backstage because the situation had become difficult for him. Many Bethel citizens protested the fact that he had permitted the use of the area, including the chaos that was created in the surrounding streets that impeded farmers from reaching their land, and that they couldn't have the milk that he produced—and countless other reasons for being upset. Yasgur's children were worried because he seemed very tired. They accompanied him behind the stage, asking that a solution be found to at least free a small passage area. It was then that some people in the audience saw what was happening. Word quickly spread among the crowd that Yasgur was on their side, that he protested why someone had put water up for sale, asking, "How can you make someone pay for water!" He himself had planted a sign in front of his house with "free water" written on it. He had also filled his car with bread, butter, and cheese to feed the crowd. He said to his fellow citizens, "If the bridge between us and the people needs to be gapped, we as adults have to do something." The organizers invited him to go up on stage and talk to the audience. He said, "I am a farmer . . . I don't know how to talk to twenty people, let alone a crowd like this. But I think you kids have proved something to the world, not only to the city of Bethel, to Sullivan County, or the state of New York. This is the biggest group of people ever gathered in one place.

Left: The crowd having fun and clapping their hands during one of the daytime performances at the festival. The concerts began in the early afternoon.

Carlos Santana

"We had no idea that there would have been so many of you and so that's why you are having problems with water, food, and so on. The producers did a huge job to make sure that everything went well for you guys and they deserve a thank you. But above all, you all proved to the world that you are half a million young kids, and I call you that because I have kids that are much older than you all, a half million youth that can stay together and spend three days full of fun and music, having nothing other than fun. May God bless you for this."

Around 2:00 P.M., the Carlos Santana band went on stage. Santana and his group—Gregg Rolie, Jose "Chepito" Areas, Mike Carabello, Michael Shrieve, and David Brown—weren't well-known outside of the Californian network. They were a young band that was getting ready to release their first album. They were strongly supported by their manager, Bill Graham, who had recommended them to Lang, convinced of their talent and possibilities. Santana, born in Mexico, moved to San Francisco at a young age and started singing in blues networks and jam sessions, where he had created his very personal blend of South American rhythms and rock.

Left: Carlos Santana and his band perform on the festival stage.

Following page: David Brown, bassist for Santana from 1966 to 1971, and Carlos Santana, while playing at the Woodstock festival.

After having heard the "Santana Blues Band" play, Bill Graham decided to put the band under contract while the guitarist's debut album was released in 1968, with the collaboration of a live album by Mike Bloomfield and Al Kooper.

Graham guaranteed the band—whose name in the meantime was shortened to Santana—a recording contract. During the days of Woodstock, the band's album still wasn't on the market yet. Not many in the crowd knew the band, but just a few minutes of a captivating mix of rock and Latin American rhythms sent the crowd into a frenzy and launched Santana into fame. They started with "Evil Ways," slow, sinuous and magical. Then, "You Just Don't Care," "Savor,"

the captivating "Jingo," "Persuasion," and followed by the song "Soul Sacrifice" that—thanks to the film—brought the wild drumming of Michael Shrieve, who was only twenty at that time, into history. Santana's finale was "Fried Neckbones and Some Home Fries."

"Soul Sacrifice," amplified in a strange way in Wadleigh's film images, swept over the entire audience, even striking those furthest from the stage who seriously strained to hear or see something in the general chaos. Santana went on stage though it was a surprise even for him. He was not, in fact, scheduled to perform. However, there was continuous chaos backstage and it was difficult to track down the artists who were scheduled to perform at the right times.

Left: Michael Shrieve, drummer for Santana, while playing at the Woodstock festival. Shrieve was only twenty years old at the time.

Above: David Brown and Michael Shrieve during the Santana performance. Shrieve revealed that he was under the influence of mescaline when he played the set.

It was at that precise moment during the festival that an artist, there by chance as an attendee, was literally thrown onto the stage. John B. Sebastian was a rock star from 1965 to 1968 who founded the legendary band Lovin' Spoonful, with whom he had conquered the charts. The band broke up and Sebastian lived nearby, between New York City and Woodstock. He went to the festival as a simple spectator, but since many of his friends were there, he also ended up backstage. At the end of Santana's performance, the rain began to fall and the next band wasn't ready to play. Plus, there were some electrical problems, so it wasn't possible to use all of the sound system. Chip Monck—worried that there would be too long of a break, which would be problematic to the flow of the concert—went to John Sebastian and asked him to perform solo with his guitar so that they wouldn't have to worry about the sound system. After all, he was John Sebastian—a true star of the time—the only one there who could capture the attention of the gigantic crowd standing in the rain. Sebastian was obviously unprepared. He hadn't even brought an instrument, so his dear friend, Tim Hardin, loaned him his guitar. Sebastian lit a joint and went on stage. He was greeted by a huge applause from the audience.

Left: John B. Sebastian gestures toward the audience at the festival. Sebastian was already famous as a member of Lovin' Spoonful.

Sebastian played five songs: "How Have You Been," "Rainbows Over Your Blues," "I Had a Dream," "Darlin' Be Home Soon" (a masterpiece, one of the most beautiful songs by Sebastian, from a love song in the Lovin' Spoonful's collection, became a song against the war, sung by the young people that left for Vietnam), and for the finale, "Younger Generation." The set was magical. It was as if Sebastian had perfectly captured the spirit of the day and the air breathed at the festival. Before the first song he said, "I simply love whoever is here. Clean up some trash as you leave and it will all go for the best." At the end of his performance, it stopped raining.

Right after, a little before 5:00 P.M., the Keef Hartley Band went on stage. They were the first British group of the festival. Hartley isn't a famous name to today's rock enthusiasts but the British drummer was already honored in the headlines as a youth when he substituted for Ringo Starr in the Rory Storm band since Starr had joined the Beatles.

He reached fame, however, when he entered in the British Blues network, and for a certain amount of time was part of the legendary group of John Mayall and the Bluesbreakers. A few months before Woodstock, he had started up the Keef Hartley Band, an ensemble inclined toward jazz rock, with Miller Anderson, Jimmy Jewell, Henry Lowther, and Gary Thain. Keef Hartley is one of the classic "mysteries" of Woodstock; an "official version" of the set doesn't exist. The information is confusing and disjointed. The band's manager refused to sign the contract for the film, and no one filmed their performance, after having been refused the two-thousand dollars more than he had requested. So only a few clips recorded by the audience exist. The most accredited version of their set list shows them playing "Spanish Fly," "She's Gone," "Too Much Thinking," "Believe in You," "Think It Over," "Rock Me Baby," and a medley with "Sinnin' for You," broken up by "Leaving Trunk" and "Just to Cry."

Left: John B. Sebastian on stage. His set was one of the most applauded of the entire festival. The singer-songwriter had perfectly captured the spirit of the festival.

Incredible String Band

Around 6:00 P.M., the Incredible String Band took the stage. One of the most loved English bands, they could be classified as psychedelic folk—a group with great success in their homeland but almost completely unknown in the United States. Besides their music—acoustic and dreamy, perfect for the first day of the festival—it wasn't exactly the most suitable for late afternoon during the second day of Woodstock. In reality, the band could have performed the night before, right after Ravi Shankar, but the rain had made that difficult, in part because of electric instruments. Joe Boyd, their manager, had insisted—since the band went on stage anyway—that they perform an acoustic set, but the musicians refused, thinking that it would have been better to perform a complete set.

Left: Christina "Licorice" McKechnie, one of the members of the Incredible String Band, joined the group in 1966, and acted as a support singer and percussionist.

Above: The Incredible String Band performs on the festival stage. From left to right: Rose Simpson, Mike Heron, Christina "Licorice" McKechnie, and Robin Williamson. The English group's performance was not included in the film.

Mike Heron, Robin Williamson, Christina McKechnie, and Rose Simpson's performance, placed on the schedule again for Saturday afternoon, was not particularly noticed by the crowd nor was it really remembered, likely due to their lack of audio and video testimony—even though the set was recorded. Ironically, the band was one of the most interesting of the time; they were pioneers in exploration of other sound cultures (today, what we would call world music) put in harmony with the undoubted psychedelic spirit and an iconic hippie look. Like other bands, their set lasted around forty minutes, and they performed six songs, all unedited: "Invocation," a spoken song; "The Letter," "Gather 'Round," "This Moment," "Come with Me," and "When You Find Out Who You Are."

Right: In this image, we can see the distance of the audience, far from the center of the festival. The picture was taken to the right of the stage on the higher part of the dip on Max Yasgur's farm.

Canned Heat

Around 7:30 P.M.—just as the sun began to set, between darkened clouds—the Canned Heat went on stage. The band had risked not participating in the festival because two days before their performance, their guitarist Harry Vestine had left the band after a fight with bassist Larry Taylor. The drummer Adolfo de la Parra had threatened to leave following the episode. Alan Wilson and Bob "The Bear" Hite had done their best to convince de la Parra to stay, and they quickly searched for a substitute for Vestine, finding one in an excellent guitarist, Harvey Mandel. So, after having held only one concert with the new guitarist precisely the first day of Woodstock, the band performed in front of the 500,000 people present. The result was extraordinary. Canned Heat's mix of blues and psychedelic music literally ignited the crowd after the "weak" performance by the Incredible String Band. Canned Heat played for about an hour, during which they performed "I'm Her Man," the beautiful "Going Up the Country," their version of "A Change Is Gonna Come" by Sam Cooke, fused with "Leaving This Town," followed by a long jam session of more than twenty minutes that was titled "Woodstock Boogie," and the concluding and legendary "On the Road Again."

Above: Adolfo de la Parra, the drummer for Canned Heat, joined the band in 1967, replacing Frank Cook.

Right: The film crew, directed by Michael Wadleigh, films Canned Heat's performance at sunset.

During the performance of the song "A Change Is Gonna Come," a young man managed to get on stage; no one from the security team stopped him or pushed him off the stage. Instead, Bob Hite greeted him and offered him a cigarette.

At 9:00 P.M., blues and rock completely took over the scene. First with Canned Heat, and then Mountain, a band that boasted a couple of vocalists and musicians on guitar and bass—Leslie West and Felix Pappalardi, respectively—along with Norman Smart on drums and Steve Knight on keyboard. Mountain performed eleven songs during their captivating set, beginning with the passionate "Blood of the Sun," which opened all of their concerts; the righteous "Stormy Monday;" "Theme for an imaginary Western," written by Jack Bruce and Pete Brown; and then "For Yasgur's Farm," "Beside the Sea," "Waiting to Take You Away," and "Dreams of Milk and Honey." Leslie West closed the band's performance with a powerful solo set of "Blind Man," "Dirty Shoes Blues," "Southbound Train," and "Mississippi Queen."

"The atmosphere was truly incredible, very beautiful," remembers Leslie West. "Our manager brought back five chickens. After the concert, around two in the morning, I remember that we lit a fire behind the stage and we cooked. Those five chickens were useful."

The Woodstock performance thrust Mountain to international success. However, thanks to several problems, it wasn't the same for Grateful Dead, who went on stage around 8:30 P.M. The first issue was purely financial. Word spread that the festival was an economic failure of epic proportions and that the band's checks from the organizers would never be able to be paid. To avoid that problem, the manager of the Grateful Dead asked for the band to be paid in advance, otherwise they wouldn't perform—similar to the Who's request. To find money in a hurry, the organizers had to practically bend over backward. The tale of how they resolved the issue is told by Joel Rosenman who claims that in order to respond to the request of the band's manager, Rosenman didn't have any other choice than to call the manager of his bank, Charlie Prince. Prince responded that there was no way to find fifty thousand dollars, since the bank was closed and the safes that held the money were locked with a timer. However, he remembered that a cashier's drawer may have possibly stayed open. He ran to the bank to find out, and then called Rosenman saying that he had the money. One problem remained: How could he get it to them? Rosenman said, "Go outside your house and wait in the garden; a helicopter will come to get it." And that's the way it was.

The Grateful Dead still had some problems—not problems with the sound (owed to the genius of their "sound magician," Owsley Stanley III, known not only for his extraordinary sound engineering, but also for his clandestine chemistry)—but the band's equipment was particularly heavy, so much so, that it put the stage's stability in danger. Also, the rain started to fall again and the stage was completely wet, making every

electric connection dangerous. The members of the band—Bob Weir, Jerry Garcia, Ron "Pigpen" McKernan, Tom Costanten, Phil Lesh, Bill Kreutzmann, and Mickey Hart— went on stage, but everything went wrong. Whenever Weir got closer to the microphone or Garcia tried to touch the guitar, there were strong electric shocks and the sound came and went. This forced the band to take long breaks between songs (one was even ten minutes long, after their classic, "Dark Star"). The set was composed of only five songs: "St. Stephen," "Mama Tried," "Dark Star," "High Time," and the final song "Turn on Your Lovelight" which all together lasted around thirty-eight minutes. Grateful Dead was known for having powerful live concerts, but the Woodstock performance is remembered by the band members themselves as their absolute worst performance. They were disconnected, probably under the influence of narcotics, and incapable of tending to technical problems on the stage. They tried to keep the band's good name against all odds, but the performance was laughable, enough for them to ask that their songs not be included on the album nor in the film.

Left and above: The Grateful Dead performing at Woodstock. According to Bob Weir, the Grateful Dead's performance was, the "worst performance of our life. Some built their career at Woodstock; we spent a decade trying to forget it!"

Traces of their performance resurfaced many years later through official recordings published in bootleg (Owsley Stanley recorded all of the band's concerts), in the album published for the fortieth anniversary, where you can listen to "Dark Star," and in the extra from the fortieth edition of the film, where excerpts of "Mama Tried" and "Turn on Your Lovelight" appear.

Rain, mud, and chaos dominated the scene. The festival schedule was significantly delayed. Lang and his crew convinced themselves that—all things considered—it wasn't bad. If they continued to keep the bands on stage all night without interruption, they would have also had more ease in maintaining calmness, continuing to hold the attention of the crowd. So, around 12:30 A.M., it was time for the most anticipated band of the entire festival: Creedence Clearwater Revival. John Fogerty, Tom Fogerty, Stu Cook, and Doug "Cosmo" Clifford were already stars. Their three albums that came out before the festival were among the biggest successes during the youth rebellion and they were an essential part of the soundtrack that the young men took to Vietnam. Some of the songs were strongly linked to that war, like in "Run through the Jungle" and "Fortunate Son." John Fogerty was one of the best authors in circulation, and the band mixed blues, soul, folk, pop, and psychedelic in an original way. Their set included eleven songs: "Born on the Bayou," to "Green River," "Ninety-nine and a Half," "Commotion," "Bootleg," "Bad Moon Rising," the rock version of "Proud Mary," the bluesy "I Put a Spell on You," and also "Night Time Is the Right Time," and finally, "Keep on Chooglin'." The audience was enthusiastic, and the applause encouraged their return on stage for the encore of "Suzie Q," which lasted ten minutes.

Right: Rain, mud, and chaos dominated the scene. The audience, however, never gave up, and they would stay in the festival area for the duration of the event.

Janis Joplin

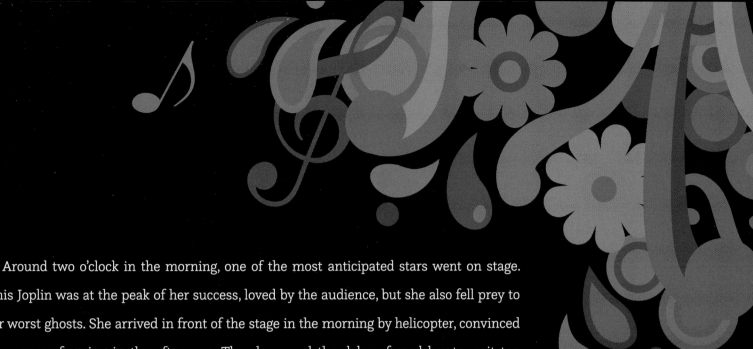

Around two o'clock in the morning, one of the most anticipated stars went on stage. Janis Joplin was at the peak of her success, loved by the audience, but she also fell prey to her worst ghosts. She arrived in front of the stage in the morning by helicopter, convinced she was performing in the afternoon. The chaos and the delays forced her to wait ten hours that she passed just being with friends, the artists from the other bands—but also drinking alcohol and injecting heroin. Fragile, emotional, extraordinary, passionate, alone and desperate, overwhelmed by success, and completely immersed in music, Janis had first won over the Bay Area and then achieved international success with the band Big Brother and the Holding Company, and in 1967 she was one of the stars at the Monterey Festival. Then the band unraveled and formed a new group in December of 1968. It was called the Kozmic Blues Band with Terry Clements, Cornelius Flowers, Luis Gasca, John Till, Richard Kermode, Brad Campbell, and Maury Baker. The large band—full of stamina and electricity—had everything it needed to achieve success. The first album with the new band, *I Got Dem Ol' Kozmic Blues Again, Mama!* was coming out. At Woodstock, Janis thought of performing a good part of those songs, just to show the crowd the new road that she had chosen. When she went on stage, she was not in the best shape, thanks to being tired and full of alcohol and drugs, but despite this, her set was full of energy. Janis performed ten songs, all enthusiastically welcomed by the audience, and with each piece she gathered more self-confidence and strength, and had fun and let herself go.

"Work me lord"

Left: The extraordinary Janis Joplin, one of the most loved stars of the time, performs at night at Woodstock.

Her set began with "Raise Your Hand," followed by "As Good as You've Been to this World." Then she surprised everyone with a beautiful blues interpretation of a Bee Gees song, "To Love Somebody," followed by a new arrangement—thanks to the stamina of the new band—of the classic "Summertime." The rhythm reclaimed energy with "Try (Just a Little Bit Harder)," followed by "Kozmic Blues," "Can't Turn You Loose," "Work Me, Lord," and for the grand finale with two encores, "Piece of My Heart" and "Ball and Chain." Janis was not satisfied with the show, despite the audience's applause, and she insisted that her performance not be included in the album or film. An album with the entire performance was published afterward, and some clips of the set appeared in the celebratory versions of the movie, and there exists the complete recording published on an unofficial DVD.

Everyone who participated in the festival agreed that the most extraordinary performance of Woodstock, both beautiful and captivating, was Sly and the Family Stone at 3:30 in the morning. It was the middle of the night at Bethel, and a good part of the audience had fallen asleep. They were tired, wet, and hungry when Sylvester "Sly" Stone and his band went on stage.

This incredible group, composed of white and black women and men, knew how to mix rock and soul like no other. They opened the road to funk and disco, and experimented with new languages in the groove of Miles Davis, but at the same time didn't forget to have fun. The group was composed of Sly, Rose Stone, Freddie Stone, Cynthia Robinson, Jerry Martini, and a rhythmic section that made history, formed by Gregg Errico and Larry Graham.

Sly was tired and worried. The delay made the band tense and nervous, and since it was dark, that didn't give the possibility to truly understand what was happening in front of the stage. They started to play "M' Lady," and little by little the sleepy audience began to stir. Then they performed "Sing a Simple Song," and the crowd began to wake up. When "You Can Make It if You Try" was over, nearly everyone was awake. The audience stood up, people who were sleeping woke up, and the crowd was going wild. At the end of "Everyday People," with its extremely strong message of peace and equality, Larry Graham remembers, "It seemed like a gigantic roar came from the audience." The sequence of the following two songs, "Dance to the Music" and "Music Lover," unleashed a frenzy. As the film showed to the world, Sly then began one of his most famous routines, "I Want to Take You Higher." He involved the crowd, with an intense call and response. The whole festival audience responded to the invitation yelling at Sly, "I want to take you higher," with a "higher" loud yell. This unanimous form of ecstasy was the most beautiful and prevalent experience of the whole festival: music, passion, emotions, and energy, rock and soul brought to an extraordinary level of spiritual and physical harmony. The band ended with the finale, "Love City" and "Stand!"—the song that was also the title of their recent 1969 album that came out a few months earlier and, pushed by their Woodstock success, sold more than three million copies.

Below: Sly Stone performed at 3:30 in the morning. Many were asleep, but after the first notes, they all woke up to join him, singing "I Want to Take You Higher."

"I want to take you higher"

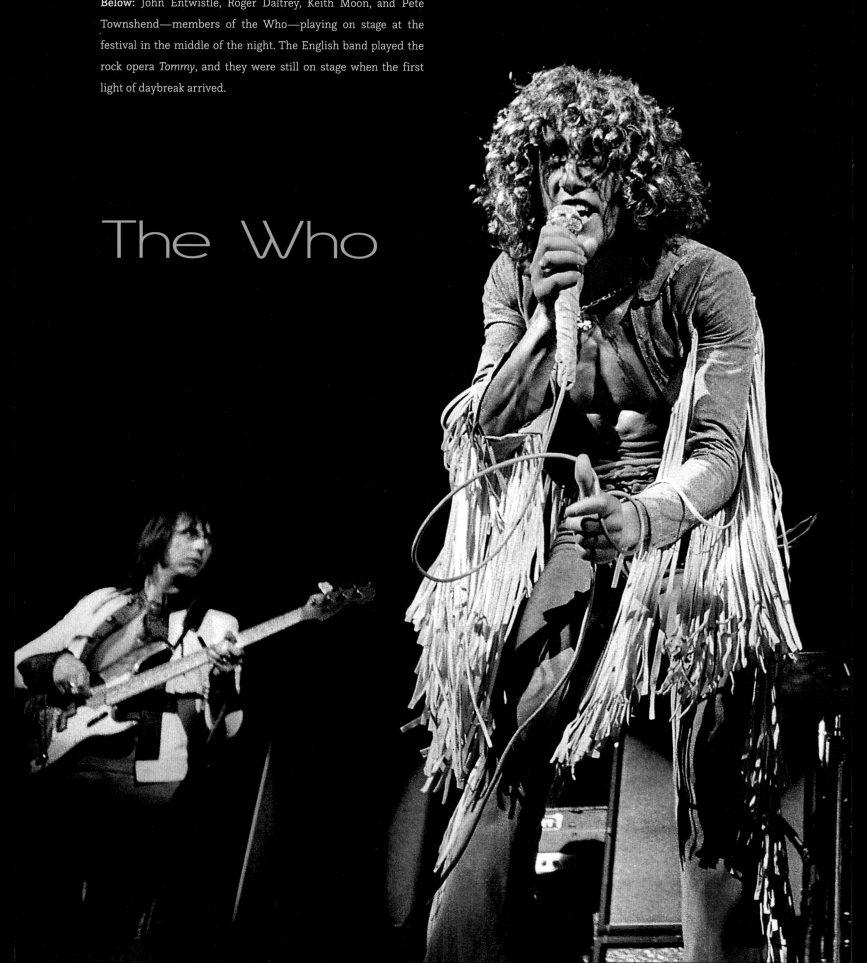

Below: John Entwistle, Roger Daltrey, Keith Moon, and Pete Townshend—members of the Who—playing on stage at the festival in the middle of the night. The English band played the rock opera *Tommy*, and they were still on stage when the first light of daybreak arrived.

The Who

At five o'clock in the morning, the Who went onstage. Even the British band had noticeable anxiety and showed little certainty in accepting to participate in the festival. They were concluding their American tour and were in the New York area, but they didn't want to stop in at Woodstock because they wanted to go home. They weren't even remotely hippies, nor were they close to the movement, and therefore weren't interested in an event like Woodstock. "Peace and love" was certainly not Townshend's favorite slogan. Despite the discontent of the four, they accepted and played well. Actually, they played really well. They stayed on stage for a little more than an hour—a span of time that forever changed their career, and was remembered as one of the best performances of the entire festival. The Who had recently released their rock opera *Tommy*, and the American tour was centered on the presentation of the songs on the album. They were in their best shape, and despite the exhaustion, the drugs (Daltrey was thought to have accidentally ingested some LSD before going on stage), and Townshend's anger, the concert was overwhelming, intense, and quite powerful.

Roger Daltrey, John Entwistle, Keith Moon, and Pete Townshend introduced the opera with some clips. They also slightly shortened the rest of the repertoire, compared to the tour, without playing pieces like "Magic Bus" or long jam sessions like "My Generation." "Heaven and Hell" (a song written by John Entwistle and never published on the official albums) was their opening song, followed by "I Can't Explain." Then the band threw themselves headfirst into the performance of a big part of *Tommy*, with "It's a Boy," "1921," "Amazing Journey," "Sparks," "Eyesight to the Blind," "Christmas," "Acid Queen," and "Pinball Wizard."

At this point, the conflict with Abbie Hoffman was confirmed (even if some stories suggest that it wasn't). Hoffman thought that there was very little political commitment at the festival, so he felt he had to go on stage at all costs and talk about John Sinclair, the head of the White Panther Party, who had been arrested by a plainclothes cop because he had a joint, and was condemned to prison for fifteen years. It was an important battle and he wanted to talk to everyone about it. Lang tried to stop him, telling him that he would have wanted him to keep his speech for the end of the Who set, but according to some witnesses, on the way to the stage from the hospital tents where he worked, he had taken at least a few different acids and was truly out of his mind. He sat on the side of the stage, and when he realized that Pete Townshend had turned for a minute to put a hand on his amplifier, Abbie got up and took the microphone. "I think it's a load of shit that John Sinclair is in prison . . ."

"Fuck off of my fucking stage!" screamed Pete Townshend.

The stories of the situation at this point vary. Townshend was already nervous and had already threatened the technicians and workers that if someone went on stage, he would have killed them with his bare hands. According to Michael Lang, Pete didn't realize that it had to do with Abbie; he simply saw that someone had taken over the microphone, and turning toward him, he accidentally hit him with his guitar. Townshend confirmed this version and Hoffman always said that he was accidentally hit. Others, however, like Henry Diltz, the official photographer of the festival, and other witnesses gathered in the Woodstock publications, maintain that Townshend's reaction was absolutely on purpose. However, the band continued playing "Do You Think It's Alright?" and at the end of the song, Townshend, even more nervous, threatened to kill anyone else who came on stage with his bare hands. Very strong evidence in favor of the "non-existence" of the incident is the fact that there are no images or videos of the presumed aggression during the most photographed and filmed festival in history.

The band continued with the performance of *Tommy*, with Moon's creative drumming, Entwistle's bass (who remained in the dark in both photos and in the film) and the extraordinary Pete Townshend who threw his microphone up in the air in a spectacular way and vertically twirled his arm in a reel on his guitar, or jumped as high as he could, playing as if he were possessed by a rock god. "There's a Doctor, "Go to the

Mirror," "Smash the Mirror," "I'm Free," "Tommy's Holiday Camp" followed one after another. Then, while the first light of daybreak appeared, the band played "We're Not Gonna Take It," followed by a stellar version of "See Me, Feel Me," with Daltrey more intense and passionate than ever. *Tommy* was finished, the crowd was electrified, everyone had listened to the Who give a performance that launched the band into the rock stratosphere.

Right: Roger Daltrey, with his historic fringe jacket, twirled the microphone during the Who's performance.

The finale exploded with "Summertie Blues," "Shakin' All Over," "My Generation" and "Naked Eye." Townshend, changing his routine from destroying his guitar, slammed it on the ground before throwing it in the crowd. None of the crowd managed to take it though because the group's roadies hurried to get it. With that performance, the history of rock changed: *Tommy* had suddenly become the center of rock at the end of the sixties and the Who had permanently won over America. Despite this, Townshend continued to maintain a negative opinion. "When I look back at the 'flower power' era, it seems dumb. I am particularly cynical in this respect because I thought it was dumb at the time . . . I didn't like Haight-Ashbury, I didn't like Abbie Hoffman, I didn't like Timothy Leary, I didn't like Woodstock."

It was therefore a little ironic that Jefferson Airplane took the stage after the Who as the sun came up. They were the aristocracy of San Francisco's new psychedelic rock and the princes of Haight-Ashbury, along with the Grateful Dead.

"Good morning, people! You saw some tough groups. Now, you will listen to some music for maniacs in the morning, believe me. It's a new dawn," said Grace Slick, introducing the band that went on stage between seven and eight o'clock in the morning. In reality, few had forgotten that extraordinary night of music, which had brought Creedence Clearwater Revival, Janis Joplin, Sly and the Family Stone, and the Who to the stage.

Right: (From left to right) Paul Kantner, an unknown girl, Marty Balin in back of her, Jack Casady with a headband in his hair, Grace Slick, some other unknown people, and standing up, Country Joe McDonald and Bill Graham, backstage at the festival.

Jefferson Airplane

Of course the members of the band hadn't slept. They were at the festival from the beginning and completely lived the experience. Now it was Grace Slick, Marty Balin, Paul Kantner, Jorma Kaukonen, Jack Casady, and Spencer Dryden's turn with Nicky Hopkins as a guest. They weren't in their best physical and mental condition but they offered a very good set, growing confidence with the time, the stage and the crowd bit by bit. They opened with "The Other Side of This Life," quickly followed by their very famous "Somebody to Love," which was already introduced on Monterey's stage. They continued with the more notable songs from their album, "3/5 of a Mile in 10 Seconds," "Won't You Try / Saturday Afternoon," the new "Eskimo Blue Day" and the more notable "Plastic Fantastic Lover." The atmosphere on stage got even

Below: Jefferson Airplane on the festival stage at dawn on the third day of the event.

warmer with "Wooden Ships," that Kantner had written with David Crosby and Stephen Stills. It was published on the following album from Airplane in a magnificent version of more than twenty minutes. It naturally blended with "Uncle Sam Blues," an antimilitarist song sung by Jorma Kaukonen. Then they performed one of the songs that became classic thanks to Woodstock, "Volunteers." This also was unpublished, destined for the album that Airplane would have released the following November. It was a strong political piece. The band had found the atmosphere and the right tone for the finale, leaving them with a version of "The Ballad of You and Me and Poonell," lasting about fifteen minutes. This was before returning on stage for three encores: "Come Back Baby," the historic "White Rabbit," and "The House at Poonell Corners."

Third Day

To maintain that the schedule was divided in days is obviously a stretch. The acts followed one another, essentially without long interruptions. Only the morning was, theoretically, deprived of music, even if it wasn't really. There was a second stage at the festival, certainly much smaller, less organized, and completely free to whomever wanted to perform. It was the "free stage," essentially run by two groups: Ken Kesey and the Merry Pranksters, who arrived on the legendary bus named "Further," and the Hog Farm. Ken Kesey was the author of the novel *One Flew Over the Cuckoo's Nest* from the time period of the big "Acid Test." Many performed on the stage but no one made it into history. The beginners and unknown artists were side by side with a few stars who, like Joan Baez and John Sebastian, performed freely for whomever was there.

Left: A boy plays the drums in one of the festival areas, which offered a "free stage" for those who wanted to perform.

Above: A girl plays the flute in a concert thrown together by the festival audience.

The "fair" element was also present since the festival had "Music and Art Fair" as a subheading. In the wooded area where they were set up, in part organized and in a larger part voluntary, stands and booths sold various items, and were visited mostly in the morning by those who weren't sleeping or who were in line to find food or make a phone call. Showers were obviously not available, so many people cleaned off the mud by going to the lake nearby. There were those who cooked, lighting small fires. There were hippie families that took care of their kids. There was generally a climate of peace and partnership despite the evident difficulties, in great part thanks to the downpour from the previous day.

Above and opposite: Images of the fair from just outside the concert area. Woodstock was a "Music and Art Fair" and there were several people who had organized sales stands, for selling merchandise like jeans (above) or handmade crafts (opposite).

Woodstock

Above: Three people hug one another with great enthusiasm. Love and friendship, a new concept of common life, was at the center of the interests for the Woodstock generation.

Above: Scenes of life like this—with a father, son, and cat—on the Woodstock field, where others slept in sleeping bags, shows how unique and exceptional in its peculiarity this festival was.

Above: Artie Kornfield, one of the organizers of the festival, plays together with a little girl in an area dedicated to percussion. The little girl plays with wind chimes surrounded by gongs and percussion of every type.

Right: Children play with a cat in the festival camping area. There were a lot of kids who, guided by their young parents, chased and played with one another, enjoying the atmosphere of freedom at Woodstock.

Above: In the woods found on Max Yasgur's farm, signs with "creative" directions were hung up to indicate which paths to follow.

Above: Joe Cocker and the Grease Band on stage at the festival. For the singer from Sheffield, the performance would transform into a real jubilation.

Between two o'clock and three o'clock P.M., the music on the main stage featured the performance of Joe Cocker and the Grease Band. Cocker, born in Sheffield, England, was more well-known in Great Britain. In the United States, he had only released a debut album, which a few weeks following the festival had reached the thirty-fifth spot on the Billboard charts. Not many knew him when he went on stage

Joe Cocker

at Woodstock with Chris Stainton, Henry McCullogh, Alan Spencer, Bobby Torres, and Bruce Rowlands. The Grease Band opened the set alone with two songs from the band Traffic: "Who Knows What Tomorrow May Bring" and "40,000 Headman." Then Cocker came on with his raspy voice, disconnecting movements, and his extraordinary emotionality. He began with his version, which became a classic, of "Dear Landlord" by

"With a little help from my friends"

Bob Dylan, followed by "Something's Coming On" and "Do I Still Figure in Your Life?" The crowd did not react in a particularly enthusiastic way but things started to change with another cover of a Traffic song that became a classic collection from Cocker, "Feelin' Alright?" followed by a new cover by Dylan, "Just Like a Woman," and especially "Let's Go Get Stoned" by Ray Charles. Then Cocker and the band performed "I Don't Need No Doctor," "I Shall Be Released," "Hitchcock Railway," and "Something to Say." Then the final twist: Cocker had put into his collection, "With a Little Help from my Friends" by the Beatles, the song sung by Ringo Starr at the beginning, of *Sgt. Pepper's Lonely Hearts Club Band*, and the song in England became a success.

When Cocker performed it on stage at the festival, he completely transformed by changing its meaning. It became the emblem of fraternity at Woodstock, of the young community. It seemed written exactly for that time, for that day. Cocker and his band transformed it into an absolute masterpiece and the crowd went crazy together with them. Cocker's career was completely changed after that performance thanks to that song, also made legendary from the film. A few months later, he published a new album in America that was a success, and a single that made it to second place. The "Mad Dogs & Englishmen" tour followed. Woodstock showed the strength and greatness of rock, the ability to change people's spirits with just a song, tell an entire story with just one song, and capture emotions, feelings, states of mind, or thoughts in only a few moments of a shared experience.

Left: Joe Cocker performing at Woodstock. The key moment of the set was the beautiful version of "With a Little Help from My Friends" by the Beatles.

Above: At the end of Joe Cocker's concert, rain began to fall again and the organizers asked the crowd to move from the stage and seek shelter. Some stayed where they were, lucky enough to have blankets.

As Cocker finished singing, dark clouds covered the festival area, and a few minutes later, a storm began. It was a downpour that would swamp everything and everyone for many hours. From the stage, the organizers asked the crowd to go look for shelter in their cars, and to get down from the scaffolding because it was dangerous. Everyone hoped that the rain wouldn't last long, but that wasn't the case; it was raining in abundance and there was strong wind. The ground had transformed into a mass of mud and there was nowhere to hide. Many began to abandon the area. The rush away from Woodstock Nation began, but many decided

to stay because the organizers chose not to end the festival and to simply wait for the return of better weather. They actually encouraged the audience to stay and for everyone to hope that the rain stopped.

"No rain" became the chant of thousands of young people who started clapping to the beat of whatever object they had available. "No rain," a prayer, an invocation, that transformed thousands of voices into one, that asked for a respite from the bad weather. At the end, the crowd got used to the rain; they acknowledged that there was no alternative, and they adapted to the situation, soaking wet and immersed in mud.

Above: Two young people use a plastic tent to cover themselves from the strong rain. Ultimately, everyone, more or less, adapted the best they could to the situation.

When the rain stopped, the situation that already appeared desperate seemed like a permanent compromise, but the spirit of Woodstock worked yet again; the sun came out to warm up the crowd and to dry their muddy clothes. Many made it to the small lake, Filippini Pond, which the organizers guaranteed they could use for water. So they took off their clothes and started to take a bath and wash themselves. Many others instead completely threw themselves in the mud, transforming the festival into a "mud fest," happily playing and taking advantage of the disaster, doing things they wouldn't have otherwise done.

Around 6:00 P.M., the music started again with Country Joe McDonald, this time accompanied by his band, Fish, formed by Barry Melton, Mark Kapner, Doug Metzner, and Greg "Duke" Dewey. The band played "Rock & Soul Music," "Thing Called Love," "Not So Sweet Martha Lorraine," "Sing Sing Sing," "Summer Dresses," "Friend, Lover, Woman, Wife," "Silver and Gold," "Maria," "The Love Machine," "Ever Since You Told Me that You Love Me (I'm a Nut)," "Crystal Blues," a refrain of "Rock & Soul Music," and to conclude again with "I-Feel-Like-I'm-Fixin'-to-Die-Rag," opened by "Fish Cheer"—this time yelled by all members of the band, one at a time.

Darkness returned to cover the wide festival area, while the rush continued in the background. Ten Years After went on stage, one of the best English blues bands of the time, led by Alvin Lee—considered at the time one of the "guitar heroes" of rock and one of the fastest guitarists in movement—with Chuck Churchill, Leo Lyons, and Rock Lee. But the technical conditions on stage—the audio system and even the crew that was recording the concert for the film (with the young Martin Scorsese as editor, squished for three days on a platform on the side of the stage)—became difficult. For Ten Years After it was decisively complicated to perform.

Left: Two young people wring out their blanket that was full of water, to dry it after the strong rain in the early afternoon.

Below: Some find shelter under a large piece of cardboard. The weather conditions on the third day of the festival brought on the maximum level of concern, but the audience did not lose the spirit of mutual support that had marked the event from the beginning.

And thanks to the humidity, the instruments easily went out of tune, and the band had to stop to retune them at the end of each song. There are no complete recordings of the English group's set, which included "Spoonful," "Good Morning Little Schoolgirl," "Hobbit," "I Can't Keep from Crying Sometimes," "Help Me," and twelve captivating minutes of "I'm Going Home." These were the only ones that the crew managed to film from the entire performance: twelve minutes that tell the story of rock, the explanation of what rock is, why it's not a genre but "a way of doing things," an attitude, a perspective.

Lee, with his performance of "I'm Going Home," did not limit himself to simply singing a song and giving substance to an extraordinary guitar solo, but he put the story of rock on stage, showcasing blues roots (with many quotes of "Boom Boom" by John Lee Hooker), those submerged in rock 'n' roll (transforming the song in "Blue Suede Shoes" and "Whola Lotta Shakin Goin' On"), transforming both blues and rock 'n' roll. In "I'm Going Home" there is agony and ecstasy, mental abandonment and physical strength. There is trance and attention, there is the desire to perform your best as a soloist, and at the same time the perfect sharing between the band and the audience. In other words, there's rock. As in the case of Joe Cocker, and also for Ten Years After, the performance of Woodstock completely changed their careers; the film then transformed them into real superstars. For those that didn't appear in the film, history remained the same: those who were famous before saw their fame continued, while those who were unown remained unkown.

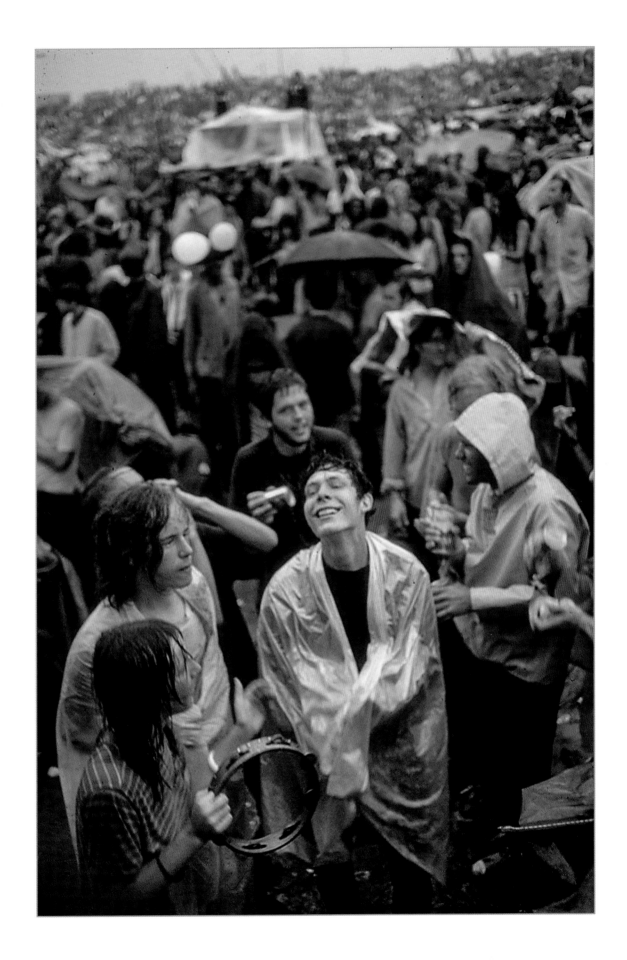

Balancing between fame and anonymity was The Band, a group destined to become famous soon enough but already enjoyed some cult status for having collaborated with Bob Dylan and become "his" band, as well as having made a debut album in 1968, *Music from Big Pink*. If it weren't for them, there probably wouldn't have been a Woodstock festival. The idea to build a high-level recording studio at Woodstock was in fact due to their presence in the area.

The five musicians—Robbie Robertson, Garth Hudson, Levon Helm, Richard Manuel, and Rick Danko—moved to Woodstock after Dylan established himself in the area, right after his "phantom" motorcycle accident. The band got a house that was nicknamed "Big Pink," and there, with Dylan, they had written, sung, and played most of the material from the legendary album *The Basement Tapes*.

Their presence in the area, that had then drawn many other musicians in, had pushed Lang to think of opening a recording studio nearby.

The group presented itself on stage after 10:00 P.M. and the audio system continued to have problems. Despite this, The Band had a magnificent performance, interpreting the "spirit of Woodstock" the best that they could.

Their mix of rock, blues, and country, on the trip between New Orleans, California, Texas, and New York, best represented the curiosity of a generation that couldn't satisfy itself by more than stories told by others. They themselves were in search of their own roots, and their own story.

Their music was hot, fun, and passionate; the fact that they grew up as "The Hawks" to then become the Dylan band in full swing of the electric revolution had thrown them into a boiling musical universe. This boiling over of creativity and music went on the stage with them.

The Band

Left: Robbie Robertson, to the left, and two other members of The Band on stage at the festival. The group had a home in Woodstock, the famous "Big Pink," where they would record their first album, and the one titled *The Basement Tapes* with Bob Dylan.

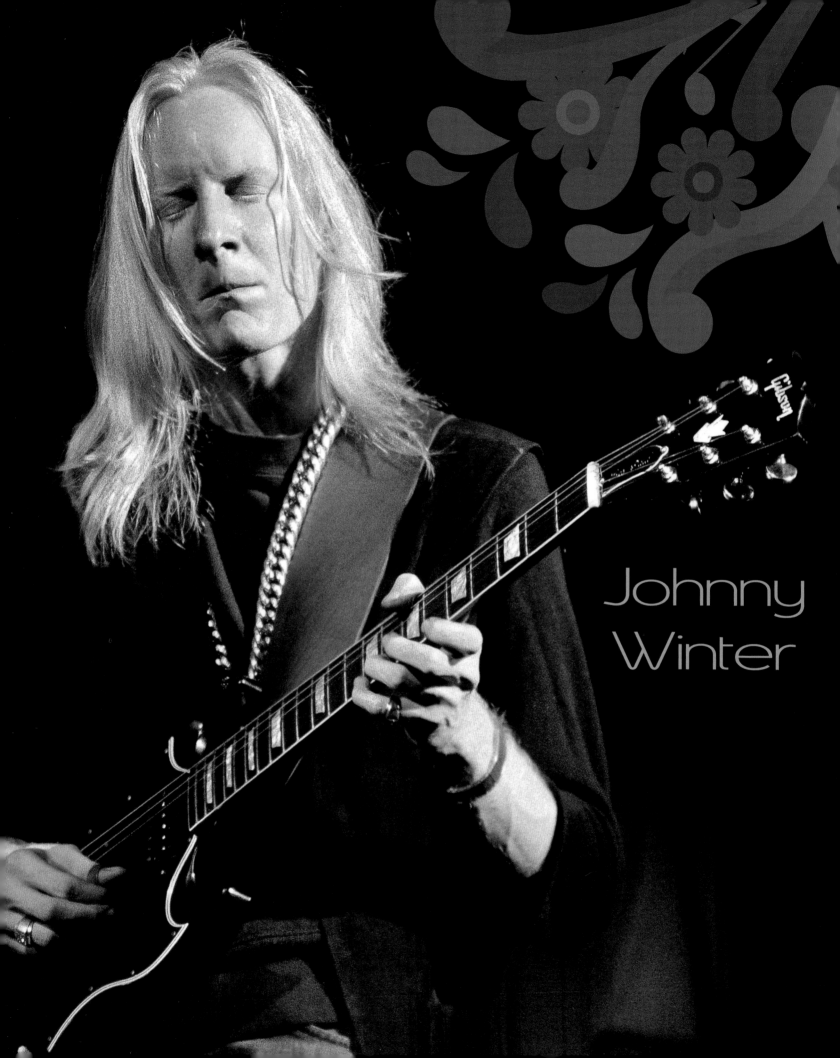

Johnny
Winter

With the name The Band, they showed off for the first time only a few months before at Winterland by Bill Graham, while their first album was released the previous month; for the group it was in that regard a "related debut."

The sequence of songs was a success: "Chest Fever," "Don't Do It," "Tears of Rage," "We Can Talk," then "The Long Black Veil," "Don't You Tell Henry," "Ain't No More Cane on the Brazos," and "This Wheel's on Fire." Then there was the wonderful finale with two songs that entered the history of music and rock, "I Shall Be Released" and "The Weight." The encore, following the applause of the audience, was "Loving You Is Sweeter than Ever" by Stevie Wonder. Although the performance was truly important, the manager of the group, Albert Grossman, blocked the set from being published in the film and on the album, thanks to a financial disagreement with the production company. Songs and videos were published in the later release of the albums and films.

Was there a better way to say goodbye to the end of the day and the beginning of a new one than to spend midnight with the band formed by Johnny Winter? Hardly. The group, composed of brothers Johnny and Edgar, Tommy Shannon, and "Uncle" John Turner, was one of the strongest blues bands in the movement. Winter was an exquisite guitarist, a true guitar and blues legend; he debuted with his first album the previous April, in the trio with Shannon and Turner, winning approval everywhere. They went on stage around midnight and set fire to the dust of "Texas Blues," with more than an hour of stimulating music. After the first four songs, "Mama, Talk to Your Daughter," "Leland Mississippi Blues," "Mean Town Blues," and "You Done Lost Your Good Thing Now" by B.B. King, blended with "Mean Mistress," brother Edgar Winter was added to the trio and, with his sax and keyboards, enriched the sound of the songs "I Can't Stand It" by Bo Diddley and "Tell the Truth," with a magnificent jazz touch. With his voice, he gave body to a beautiful version of "Tobacco Road." The finale, perfect for a big night party at Woodstock, was "Johnny B. Goode" by Chuck Berry.

Left: Blues guitarist Johnny Winter during his performance at Woodstock. "I went up on stage sleepy, I put the guitar in my arms, and started playing," he said.

As had happened the previous evening, the delay brought the superstars, the most anticipated bands, to perform at the end of the night. Blood, Sweat & Tears went on stage around 1:30 A.M. Technically counting, it was already the fourth day of the festival, August 18. The band was one of the groups with more success at the time. They had made two albums that climbed the charts, and two smash hits: "Spinning Wheel" and "You've Made Me Feel So Very Happy." One of the founders, Al Kooper, had already left the group. They were almost an orchestra, composed of David Clayton-Thomas, Bobby Colomby, Lew Soloff, Jerry Halligan, Jim Fielder, Steve Katz, Fred Lipsius, and Chuck Winfield. The band blended rock, blues, jazz, pop, soul, R & B, and even some elements of classical music. It was a perfect example of the creative direction that rock was taking at the end of the sixties and what would have soon enough take it to the birth of prog. The songs performed by Blood, Sweat & Tears were "More and More," "Just One Smile," "Something's Coming On," "More Than You'll Ever Know," "Spinning Wheel," "Sometimes in Winter," "God Bless the Child," "And When I Die," and the finale, "You've Made Me So Very Happy." It was not a particularly exciting set. In the words of Fred Lipsius, it was the worst that the group did in their entire career, especially because, in his words, David Clayton-Thomas sang off-key for a good part of the concert. It's hard to confirm if it was truly like that because the band's manager couldn't agree on the compensation for the film and album, and the group's set was not recorded. The four songs that were recorded actually aren't bad. Their presence at the festival was decisively short: they came, they played, and they left in about two hours.

If the last night of the festival was rich in music, the best contributor maybe came from a group that had formed recently: the quartet "all stars," made up of David Crosby, Stephen Stills, Graham Nash, and Neil Young. Crosby came from the Byrds, Stills and Young from Buffalo Springfield, and Nash from the English Hollies. Each one of them had already had success.

Left: David Clayton-Thomas, singer from Blood, Sweat & Tears, during their concert. The manager of the band never reached an agreement with the organizers, so the recordings were never put into the film.

Following pages: Graham Nash and David Crosby on the Woodstock stage during their performance. Crosby, Stills & Nash play for the first time together in 1968 at Woodstock, which was their first real concert.

Crosby, Stills & Nash

The trio of Crosby, Stills & Nash had already released an album the May before the festival and shortly after, Neil Young joined them. The performance at Woodstock was their second performance in public. The long set was divided in two parts: an acoustic one and an electric one. This was to give completeness to an extremely rich and diverse musical presentation and to express their different personalities in play. Neil Young doesn't appear in the movie because he didn't want to be filmed, and the presence of the workers strongly annoyed him. It was an important occasion. They were presenting themselves to the public for the first time. They made themselves known in the musical environment as an "ensemble," searching for the definite confirmation of their status and beginning a new period for each one of them.

The concert was opened by an extraordinary version of "Suite: Judy Blue Eyes," written by Stillis, that perfectly emphasized the vocal melodies of the band. Abilities that were word for word glorified by the following song, a magic rereading of "Blackbird" by the Beatles. Then the trio performed another three songs from the first album, "Helplessly Hoping," "Guinnevere," "Marrakesh Express," and the unedited "4+20," before coming together with Neil Young, with whom they played "Mr. Soul" by the Buffalo Sprinfield, "I'm Wondering," and "You don't have to cry." So, after being joined by the rhythmic section composed of Dallas Taylor and Greg Reeves, the electric part of the concert began with "Pre-Road downs," "Long Time Gone," "Sea of Madness," and "Wooden Ships." It was a real triumph. It was both the baptism and the consecration of a band that from that moment would go on to dominate the rock scene. When called back to the stage, they brought the magic of "Find the Cost of Freedom" and closed out with "49 Bye Byes." Crosby, Stills, Nash and Young were all at Woodstock and they were Woodstock: they were a group of four different personalities very different from one another. They had formed a community, producing incredible vocal harmonies, imagining new worlds and living the moment in the most complete way. The film, not on purpose, was centered on them, using their music and their images as the music and image of the festival.

Right: Neil Young at Woodstock. The guitarist did not like the presence of Michael Wadleigh's crew on stage, so he asked not to be filmed and to not appear in the film.

"Find the cost of freedom"

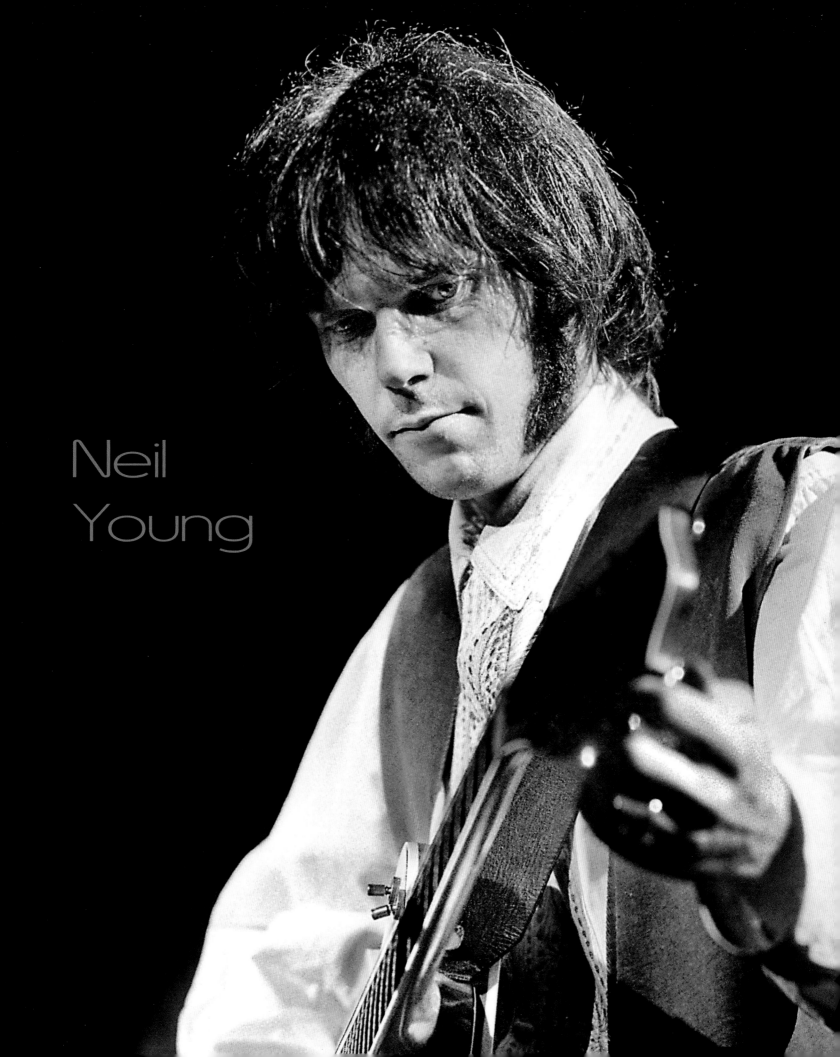

Neil
Young

Fourth Day

Above: A line of young people moving away from the Woodstock festival area, walking next to a puddle of water and mud.

By now it was the dawn of the fourth day. This day was not supposed to be there because the festival was supposed to close at night. Instead, the music continued. Most of the 500,000-person crowd were already on the road home. There were tens of thousands of people still in front of the stage, waiting for the sun to come up. The Paul Butterfield Blues Band greeted the new day. An excellent harmonic player, and faithful to the blues of Chicago, Butterfield had had a lot of success with his band in the previous years (it was the band from the first electric concert of Bob Dylan at Newport in 1965 and among the Monterey festival stars in 1967). After Mike Bloomfield and Elvin Bishop abandoned the group, he could no longer find a balance and record with the same appreciation.

Above: Mike Bloomfield and Al Kooper, pictured with Ted Harris on the keyboard, play the morning of the fourth day with the Paul Butterfield Blues Band.

The Woodstock performance may have been the last by the group. At the time, they were profoundly renewed and broadened with a winds section, in the furrow of Blood, Sweat & Tears and Chicago. Next to Bloomfield now was Ron Hicks, Philip Wilson, Howard Feiten, Steve Madaio, Keith Johnson, Trevor Lawrence, Gene Dinwiddie, and a very young David Sanborn. The set was compact and fun. The band played "Born Under a Bad Sign," "No Amount of Loving," "Driftin' and Driftin'," "Morning Sunrise," which was adapted at the time, "All in a Day," "Love March," and "Everything's Gonna Be Alright," all to much audience applause.

Right after them, it was time for one of the most unique groups of the time period, Sha Na Na. Few today remember the band formed by Joe Witkin, Jocko Marcellino, Donny York, Rob Leonard, Alan Cooper, Dennis Greene, Dave Garrett, Richie Joffe, Scott Powell, Henry Gross, Bruce Clarke III, and Elliot Cahn, but the New York band was one of the most original and fun groups on the rock scene. They were "revivalists." They had a collection essentially made of rock 'n' roll, rockabilly, and doo-wop. They presented their music with theatricality, irony, and a spectacularity that truly no one else had. Dressed in lamé with slicked hair, Sha Na Na sang magnificently and had perfected their choreography. They were able to wake up even those who were fast asleep at 7:30 in the morning when "they invaded" the Woodstock stage to present "Get a Job," "Come Go with Me," "Silhouettes," the teen pop song "Teen Angel," a rock 'n' roll song by Elvis Presley called "Jailhouse Rock," a surf song by the Surfaris, called "Wipe Out," the classic and romantic, "Blue Moon," the beautiful "(Who Wrote) The Book of Love," and "Little Darling," before launching into the grand finale with "At the Hop," "Duke of Earl," and the reprise of "Get a Job."

Left: A girl from the festival staff begins to clean up the concert area. Cleaning up the enormous mass of trash already began during the third day of the festival.

Jimi Hendrix

Sha Na Na came to Woodstock, thanks to Jimi Hendrix's advice. He saw them play a few weeks earlier at the Scene Club, in New York City, and they became his support band. On the fourth day at nine o'clock in the morning, Hendrix and his new band, Gypsy Sun and Rainbows—made up of Billy Cox, Mitch Mitchell, Larry Lee, Juma Sultan, and Gerardo Velez—closed out the festival.

Hendrix presented nineteen songs in a set that lasted more than two hours. The list included a brief "Introduction" followed by "Message to Love," "Getting My Heart Back Together Again/Hear My Train a-Coming," "Spanish Castle Magic," "Red House," "Mastermind," sung by Larry Lee, "Lover Man," "Foxy Lady," "Beginning/Jam Back at the House," with a brief solo by Mitch Mitchell, "Izabella," "Gypsy Woman," also sung by Larry Lee, "Fire," "Voodoo Child (Slight Return)," "Stepping Stone," "Star-Spangled Banner," "Purple Haze," a "Woodstock Improvisation," all before the finale with "Villanova Junction" and the inevitable "Hey Joe."

The performance, as much as it was intense and engaging, was not one of Hendrix's best, especially the part passed onto history thanks to the film, or rather the performance of the American anthem, "Star-Spangled Banner," which transformed into a very powerful cry against the war. The band was just beginning. They had tried playing only a few times together. The new group, with a second guitarist and two percussionists, was decidedly unpopular with Hendrix's producer, Eddie Kramer. In the final mix of the instruments to be used were still the bass and drum, just like in the group Experience; part of the new sound of the group was lost, and the other musicians heard themselves only in the background.

Left and above: Jimi Hendrix performing what concluded the long series of concerts at the Woodstock festival. You can see bassist Billy Cox behind him. At the time of Hendrix's performance, there were still a few tens of thousands of people at Woodstock, and the festival area was emptied out, for the most part.

Despite the flaws, the set list called for good, tested pieces, and some new songs. Hendrix was looking for new roads, as he notes in the wonderful "Woodstock Improvisation" in which he plays alone and tries to give body to a relentless creative flow. The guitar, therefore, became a half and an end, an instrument and a cult, a desired object and a map that Hendrix looked for constantly—his island. No one, before and after Hendrix, had used the guitar in a similar way.

His style, unmatched and inimitable, put together spectacularity and invention; his way of playing married technique and innovation. Every note of his solo seemed to be there for a specific reason, for an inescapable need. It wasn't only fascination and mystery but also expression of an interior reality that extraordinarily saw the light. On the Woodstock stage, in which Hendrix had requested to be the closing act, the guitarist was free to play as much as and however he wanted. This freedom is maybe the most beautiful element of a performance that, by putting together the last piece of that incredible event, has passed into history.

Right: Jimi Hendrix played the fourth morning of the festival, surrounded by the crowd. "It's strange but when we went up on stage, there were barely fifteen thousand people there," stated the guitarist, talking about the performance.

"Star-Spangled Banner"

Carlos Santana

"The Woodstock festival in 1969 was one of those rare moments in which human energy managed to alter reality." Fifty years passed from that August of 1969 and Carlos Santana still remembers those days, not with nostalgia but with passion. At that time, the young Carlos was a promising guitarist who came from the San Francisco Bay at the beginning of the sixties. He was in love with blues and the new rock scene. He was thrown on that stage, full of energy and his music.

And from that moment on, the whole world learned of his music and his guitar. "For me it was the beginning of a dream, the proof that everything we dreamed of at that time was true, was possible.

Right: Carlos Santana at a concert in 2016. The noteworthy guitarist won multiple Grammys and recorded thirty-one albums with both the band and as a soloist, and another seven live albums.

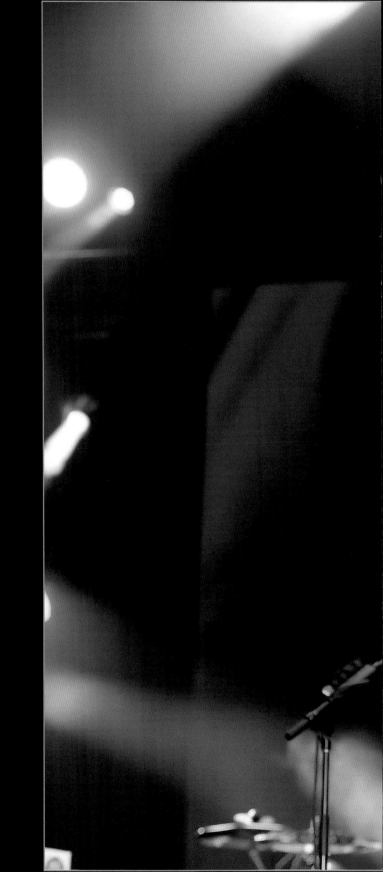

We were doing it, all together, as artists on the stage and the crowd in front us. If something was left? Of course, everything that was planted remained. And we, in those days, planted a lot of love."

Carlos Santana was already a celebrity in his various Californian networks. He performed more times in the San Francisco Bay and at Bill Graham's historic Fillmore. When he came on stage at Woodstock, he certainly wasn't a star. For him, everything changed after that festival. "It was actually thanks to the film. It threw our image in an extraordinarily legendary way. It amplified a lot, not only the already powerful course of the event, but it contributed to make it become a global festival, to spread music and the message to every part of the world. And for me, I said it many times, it was a trampoline that launched me high up, and I never came down from that height."

Had you ever felt the same emotion that you felt when you went on that stage?

"You can't ever feel the same emotion twice. Every moment of our life is unique and unrepeatable. Of course, as musicians we are lucky. We are greeted by the energy of millions of people every time that we go up on stage. And to retransmit that energy to whomever is listening to it. No, I didn't feel that same emotion but many emotions likewise extraordinary."

What made that festival so unique?

"Everything, really. First of all, the crowd that were gathered there, hugging one another, supporting each other for three days in an absolute self-government

situation. And the music, that put the best emotions in movement. The festival was a total mess and yet it all worked out. Then, for me, it was a sensational performance, also because when I went on stage, I was under the influence of mescaline. As soon as I arrived, I met Jerry Garcia and I asked him what time they were expected on stage. He said to me, 'You guys play after us, and we will be on stage around two in the morning.' I thought I had a lot of time available, so I took mescaline. But shortly after, someone came to tell me 'You guys are going on stage, you guys are playing now or you guys aren't playing anymore.' And so we did."

Many indicate Woodstock as the arrival point of the sixties. After Woodstock, dreams were shattered …

"I don't think it was truly like that. The energy of those days was reflected for a long time, not only on who participated in that event but also on who saw the film, who knew what happened. For us, everything began with Woodstock. My first album came out a few months later in November, and right away, the band was an international hit. We came off that stage and were swamped with requests. Rock music took on a different meaning that it didn't have up until then. And for many verses it was Hendrix's set to prove it."

Did you meet Hendrix at any other times?

"I saw him play one time, a few months before Woodstock at Santa Clara Fairgrounds in San José. It may have been the most wonderful concert that I saw, but I didn't know him. We met each other at Woodstock. Then I saw him play again at Berkeley Community

Center in 1970 and we talked a little. He was a star, I was taking my first steps but he said that I had a 'good choice of notes.' You could see that he needed something that he couldn't manage to find. But it was incredible because he truly had everything: the talent, communication skills, the vision, and the willpower. And success." Many years later, in 1994, Santana was on stage at Woodstock II. At that time, they hoisted Jimi Hendrix's sister onstage.

"Yes, it was an exciting moment. I knew that she wanted to talk to the crowd, so I offered for her to come up on stage and share it with us. The sky was gray, it rained continuously in those days, but when she came up on stage, everything suddenly changed; it stopped raining, the sky cleared and really there was only a cloud left that looked like an angel right above the stage. Everyone saw it. It was a magical moment." At that time she wanted to pay tribute to Hendrix bringing back "Star-Spangled Banner."

"Yes, we had prepared a video clip of Hendrix at Woodstock when he played that incredible version of the American anthem to show before our concert. We had also selected other images from the sixties, from the Vietnam War, and peace rallies. I was ready to say that we had Hendrix's spirit with us, but the festival lawyers stopped us because at the time, there were tons of legal troubles over Hendrix's inheritance and copyrights between his producer Alan Douglas and Jimi's dad, Al Hendrix. In other words, as incredible as it seems, we were at Woodstock and we couldn't celebrate Hendrix. When his sister went up on stage and spoke, I

felt much better. I thought, 'Now I can play my music.' I felt at peace, in a magical and perfect state. Hendrix was truly with us, regardless of the lawyers…"

What difference is there between Woodstock of 1969 and the festival of 1994?

"It is impossible to make comparisons. Two completely different time periods, different generations, different dreams. The two concerts told us the same thing though, that is that hundreds of thousands of people, if they want to achieve something important, good, they can really do it. Because the young people still needed the same things that we needed." Do big rock gatherings still make sense today? "Why not? If people want to stay together and share emotions and energy, this can only be positive. Of course, there is business behind everything, too much money going around and little spirituality among those who organize the festivals. But it's always been that way. Then the crowd comes, there's music, and nothing else matters."

Are you ever nostalgic about the sixties? "No, I am not the type that lives through nostalgia. I think what life can offer tomorrow is always fantastic. The music from those years talked about this. Hendrix's music also said this, that everyone has possibilities and that you don't have to do anything other than move and try to achieve your dreams. it is the dream of the sixties but also of the future. Peace, love, and music is surely a slogan that never went out of style. Actually, nowadays it's used more often."

Richie Havens

Richie Havens was a nice guy and an extraordinary musician. His life was deeply marked by the Woodstock festival, which gave him enormous fame all over the world, especially thanks to the film. Havens was one of the rising personalities from the new folk of Greenwich Village when he was invited to perform at the festival. "The Woodstock festival could almost not have been because none of us were truly able to get up to there," he remembered years later. "The hotel where we were placed was about six miles far from the concert location, and there was only one street to get there, but it was completely blocked by the crowd and parked cars. We were convinced we had taken a trip for nothing and that we wouldn't be able to perform. But it wasn't like that. The organizers rented a helicopter and it went back and forth between the hotel and the festival, bringing everyone that it could. We were squashed inside, myself, two musicians that were with me, the guitars, and the percussions. After a few minutes, we were on top of that extraordinary and enormous lively crowd. It felt unbelievable to us. In the first afternoon, there was only me, my band, and Tim Hardin behind the stage. At a certain point, Michael Lang came to me and desperately asked for us to go on stage and play. We were not even all there. We were still missing the bassist. I was expected on stage much later; I was fifth on the schedule but the situation was such that I couldn't say no. I went on stage and started playing. After a half hour, I said goodbye and tried to get off but they gestured for me to keep going. I did a few more pieces and tried to get off stage again but they still told me to continue. At that point, I improvised "Freedom" with the others. That word came in my head because it was truly what we were all looking for. I sang it rhythmically with the guitar tuned on one pitch, and my foot tapped the ground. It came naturally to blend it together with the words from 'Motherless Child,' a beautiful song that I hadn't sung for years. The more we moved forward, the more emotions came up. We thought we were in perfect harmony with the audience, that the atmosphere created was unique. It was an astounding experience."

Left: Richie Havens, live in New York, in 2009. The American musician, who passed away in 2013, was one of the most respected blues and folk singer-songwriters during the sixties.

Neil Young

The most famous "Woodstock musician ghost" was Neil Young. "Ghost," not because he wasn't there, but because he decided not to be seen. "We were very excited, enthusiastic, not only because there were a lot of noteworthy musicians at the festival but especially because there were also so many people—500,000 people. We were a generation in movement, we were someone. And we were making a difference. The music was there; it wasn't a product or 'content.' The music was life, it was an essential part of everything. The music is a stream, going forward and backward. You sing and the people listen. Just one thing and it's beautiful. What I didn't like was the film crew. I hated those cameramen on stage. It was a distraction. They were everywhere. I said, 'Don't come near me. I have a heavy guitar. Don't let me see you,' and they kept their distance. I was skinny, not a threat, but I was rather nervous. I was in a situation that I didn't like. So I didn't let myself be seen."

Left: Neil Young in Los Angeles in 2012. The guitarist was the most famous "ghost musician" of the festival.

Paul
Kantner

"We went to Woodstock like we normally did at that time, without thinking about it. But it was quickly clear that it didn't have to do with something like the others. It was a place where chaos and anarchy reigned but where on the contrary to what you would usually think, chaos and anarchy worked to perfection. The climate was like rafting, where you go in a canoe, looking to block hazards. That is, at Woodstock, the people were not worried about problems or dangers; they only thought about how to avoid them and how to give a hand to others to do just as much."

Right: Paul Kanter of Jefferson Airplane, who passed away in 2016, performing live in New York in the nineties.

Ralph Towner

"The Woodstock experience was incredible, to which we almost participated by chance. Paul Winter called me, saying that he needed some musicians. I responded that myself, Glen, and Colin Walcott were available. We went to Woodstock with Tim Hardin. We thought we had to play in a small folk festival while we got closer to Bethel in the car. But when we understood that to go on stage we had to take a helicopter, some doubts started coming over us. We arrived in flight and seeing all of those people from up high was truly a shock. Playing was amazing and it certainly didn't happen to me again, to play like that in front of such a big audience. But the most important thing about the festival wasn't the music, but the fact that it was truly happening, that the people were there in peace, and that everyone had a positive spirit. There was harmony and good will and everything was spontaneous. No one thought that something like this could happen, and obviously I believe that it's not possible for it to repeat itself because it wasn't planned; it happened in a natural way. After the music, the festivals even changed. Everything became a matter of money. It was deprived of that magic that Woodstock had."

Above: Ralph Towner, legendary guitarist from the band Oregon, on the Woodstock stage, where he is accompanied by Tim Hardin.

"To be completely honest, I would say that Woodstock changed my life. I didn't realize it right away but the effect was extraordinary. I realized that it was something bigger when I arrived in a helicopter above the area and saw that sea of people that were in front of the stage. The band was already ready. I arrived and started singing. I don't think there was anyone else available at that time. We started, and little by little we understood the spirit of the matter. To tell the truth, the others were high on acid, but I only discovered it later. I was the only one not under any influence. But it was very nice, especially when I started singing 'With a Little Help from My Friends.' I knew I had affected someone's heart, which for me was fantastic."

Joe Cocker

Above: Musician Joe Cocker performing live in concert.

Bob Weir

"Woodstock was a double experience for us. The first was the festival, being together with other musicians, lots of young people, and truly being happy together. There was a wonderful atmosphere both behind and in front of the stage. The second was the concert, and ours was without a doubt the worst concert in our history. It rained a lot and continued to do so. The stage was literally impassable. The sound technician had tried to put the wiring back but the results of his work were terrible. Every time that I touched the electric guitar, I got shocked. I had become a conductor. There was a huge blue shock when I touched the microphone and it jumped behind the shock. A terrible experience."

Right: Bob Weir from the Grateful Dead performing live in concert, in 2016.

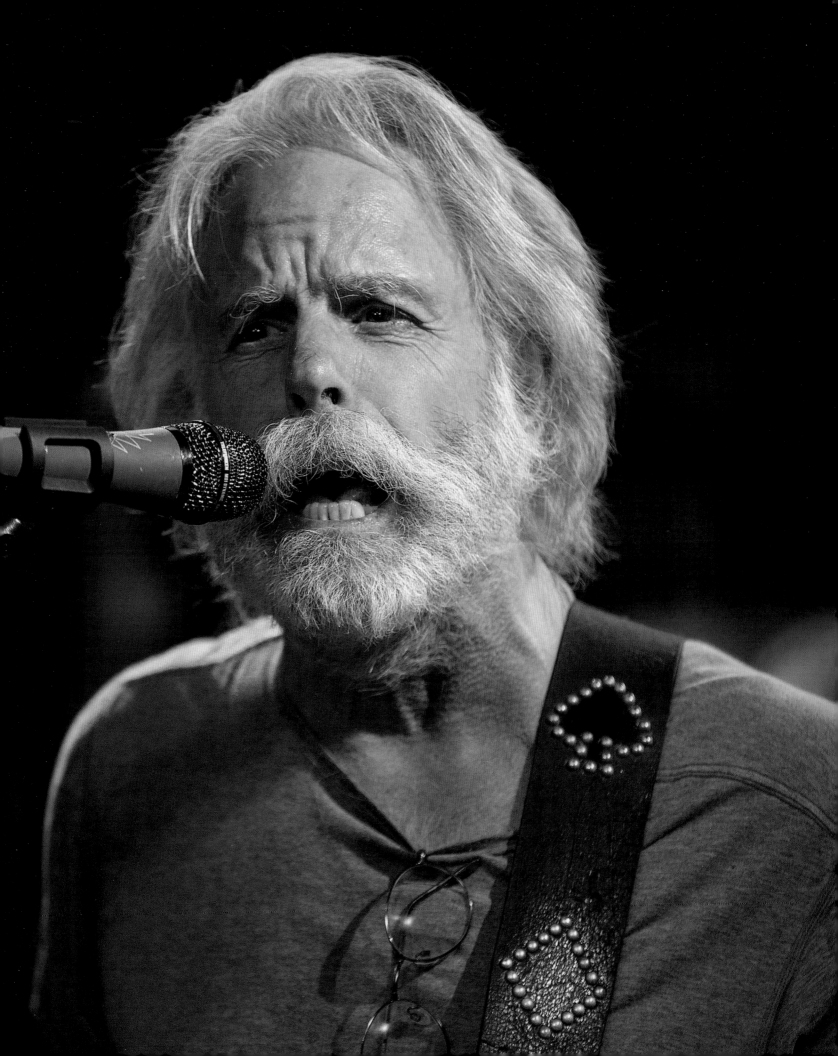

Roger Daltrey

"It was truly an unbelievable experience. There was mud everywhere, nothing to eat, the humidity went into your bones, and for a singer, the risk of losing your voice was real. And then everything that you drank had something in it. It was 'spiked' with any substance. So, to tell the truth, at a certain point I didn't know who I was or what band I was a part of. But the atmosphere among us was remarkable. We were staying at the Holiday Inn. Jefferson Airplane, Jimi Hendrix, Grateful Dead, and Joe Cocker were also there. Every once in awhile, someone disappeared to go play and then didn't come back. And behind the stage there was more chaos with musicians, managers, agents, and promoters. Some argued with the organizers because they wanted to be paid. We also wanted to be paid before we played and we managed to do so. So we went on stage, and on stage the chaos, if possible, was even greater. Almost nothing worked and it was impossible to hear what I was singing. What saved us was the sunrise behind the audience while I sang 'See Me, Feel Me.' It was the most beautiful light show that we could have ever imagined."

Right: Musician Roger Daltrey performing live in concert with the Who in 2015, in London.

Grace Slick

"We were very interested in the festival. We thought it could be an 'East Coast' version of Monterey but the reality was very different.

"We had to go on stage at 9:00 P.M. and they had to come get us at the Holiday Inn with the helicopter because all of the streets were blocked. The helicopter came to get us at 6:30 P.M. but we played at 7:00 in the morning! We spent the whole time behind the stage and they continued to tell us, 'It's not your turn yet.'

"So we passed the time by smoking something and drinking wine, chatting with other musicians that were around, and trying not to put our feet in the mud.

"Around 10:30 P.M., someone came to tell us, 'You are going on stage in an hour,' but that obviously wasn't true. It was a difficult situation. You couldn't even go to the bathroom, and there wasn't much to eat. We finally went on stage at 7:00. We were dead tired. I stayed awake the whole night. I was also very cold, because not thinking of this possible situation, I came with my light California clothing. We saw all of the people and started playing. At the end, it went rather well."

Right: Grace Slick, singer from Jefferson Airplane and Jefferson Starship, in a recent picture.

The Author

Ernesto Assante has collaborated with numerous weekly and monthly Italian and international publications, including *La Repubblica*, *Epoca*, *L'Espresso*, and *Rolling Stone*. He is the author of books on music criticism, a few of which were co-written with his colleague Gino Castaldo. In 2005, the two created "Lezioni di Rock. Viaggio al Centro della Musica" ("Lessons in Rock. A Voyage into the Heart of Music"). Among his many publications about music are *Legends of Rock*, *Masters of Rock Guitar*, *5 Seconds of Summer*, *The Milestones of Rock & Roll*, and *U2: Past, Present, Future*.

Image credits

Brimming with creative inspiration, how-to projects, and useful information to enrich your everyday life, Quarto Knows is a favorite destination for those pursuing their interests and passions. Visit our site and dig deeper with our books into your area of interest: Quarto Creates, Quarto Cooks, Quarto Homes, Quarto Lives, Quarto Drives, Quarto Explores, Quarto Gifts, or Quarto Kids.

Published in 2018 by becker&mayer! books, an imprint of The Quarto Group, 11120 NE 33rd Place, Suite 201, Bellevue, WA 98004 USA.
www.QuartoKnows.com

becker&mayer! books titles are also available at discount for retail, wholesale, promotional, and bulk purchase. For details, contact the Special Sales Manager by email at specialsales@quarto.com or by mail at The Quarto Group, Attn: Special Sales Manager, 401 Second Avenue North, Suite 310, Minneapolis, MN 55401 USA.

Originally published as *Woodstock '69: The Rock and Roll Revolution* by White Star Publishers®

WS White Star Publishers® is a registered trademark property of White Star s.r.l.

© 2018 White Star s.r.l.
Piazzale Luigi Cadorna, 6
20123 Milan, Italy
www.whitestar.it

18 19 20 21 22   5 4 3 2 1

ISBN: 978-0-7603-6325-6

Author: Ernesto Assante
Design: Maria Cucchi
Editorial: Valeria Manferto de Fabianis

Printed, manufactured, and assembled in Milan, Italy, 08/18.
Distributed by:
Quarto UK, The Old Brewery
6 Blundell Street, London N7 9BH, UK
Allen & Unwin
30 Centre Rd, Scoresby VIC 3179, AUS

305524